THOUGHT FIELD THERAPY

Robin Ellis

authorHOUSE®

AuthorHouse™ UK Ltd.
500 Avebury Boulevard
Central Milton Keynes, MK9 2BE
www.authorhouse.co.uk
Phone: 08001974150

©2011. Robin Ellis. All rights reserved
No part of this book may be reproduced, stored in
a retrieval system, or transmitted by any means
without the written permission of the author.

First published by AuthorHouse 3/11/2011

ISBN: 978-1-4567-7376-2

This book is printed on acid-free paper.

Because of the dynamic nature of the Internet, any Web addresses or links contained in this book may have changed since publication and may no longer be valid. The views expressed in this work are solely those of the author and do not necessarily reflect the views of the publisher, and the publisher hereby disclaims any responsibility for them.

Apart from the TFT-specific content of this book, readers should note that the information given about professional standards (and reference to health professionals and services) apply to the practice of Thought Field Therapy within the United Kingdom. I'm sure that the same standards would apply the world over, but regulation of therapeutic practice is variable. Do make sure that if you are in practice elsewhere, you consult the regulatory framework that applies in your country.

For Mary

Contents

CHAPTER 1	**THE TFT PROTOCOL**	
	1. Algorithms.	2
	2. The TFT Architecture	3
	3. Using the SUD scale effectively	4
	4. How to give a TFT Treatment	11
	5. Further Ideas	25
	6. The Protocol Summary	27
	7. Case study from student	30
CHAPTER 2	**PSYCHOLOGICAL REVERSAL**	
	1. What is Psychological Reversal?	33
	2. Types of PR and their Correction	35
CHAPTER 3	**FINDING THE PROBLEM THOUGHT FIELDS**	
	1. Basic TFT principles	39
	2. Finding the core issue	41
	3. Looking for every thought field	44
	4. Questions & Case Studies from students.	48
CHAPTER 4	**ANXIETY AND FEAR**	
	1. What is Anxiety?	59
	2. What is Fear?	60
	3. Understanding Anxiety & Fear	61
	4. Treating Anxiety & Fear	65

CHAPTER 5 PANIC ATTACKS AND PANIC DISORDER

1. What are Panic Attacks? 74
2. What is Panic Disorder? 76
3. Understanding Panic Disorder 77
4. Treating Panic Disorder 78

CHAPTER 6 TRAUMA AND PTSD

1. What is Acute Stress Disorder? 81
2. What is Post Traumatic Stress Disorder? 83
3. TFT and Traumatic Stress 84
4. Treating Traumatic Stress 86
5. Case Study and Studies from Students 90

CHAPTER 7 GRIEF

1. What is Grief? 107
2. Treatment for Bereavement 108
3. Treatment for Divorce or Separation 111

CHAPTER 8 ANGER & RAGE

1. What is the Difference? 114
2. Understanding Anger & Rage 115
3. Treating Anger and Rage 115
4. Case Study 117

CHAPTER 9 PHOBIAS

1. What is a phobia? 119
2. Understanding Phobias and Traditional Treatments 120

	3. Treating Phobias	122
	4. Treating Phobias Associated with Past Trauma	126
	5. Case Study and Studies from Students	129

CHAPTER 10 ADDICTIONS & OCDs

1. Presentation — 138
2. First contact with your client — 143
3. Treatment of urge/desire to indulge — 145
4. Psychological Reversal and the addictive force — 146
5. Addressing both sides of the problem — 147
6. Further treatments to combat the addiction — 150
7. Case Study and Studies from Students — 157

CHAPTER 11 DEPRESSION

1. What is Depression? — 163
2. Treating Depression — 165
3. TFT Treatment for Depression — 166

CHAPTER 12 PHYSICAL PAIN

1. What is Pain? — 169
2. Treating Physical Pain — 170

CHAPTER 13 THERAPY WITH CHILDREN

1. The Legal Issues. — 173

Chapter 14   Treating Children

1. How to use TFT for treating a Child   178
2. "Beware of the Child" - Examples & Case Studies   179
3. Working with Groups of Children   187

Chapter 15   Professional Standards

1. The Complementary Medical Practitioner   190
2. Knowing your Limitations   195
3. The Risks and Duty of Care   197
4. The Need to Provide a Safe Environment   199
5. Professional Indemnity Insurance   201
6. Keeping Records   201
7. Confidentiality   203
8. At-a-glance guide   206

Foreword

In Thought Field Therapy, The Definitive Guide to Successful Practice, Robin and Ian have done a meticulous job of instruction, guidance and feedback that reflect their years of experience in health care and their high level of skill in the application of this powerful healing modality. It clearly represents their years of expertise in supporting new TFT practitioners, leading them to professional and successful application.

They are pioneers of TFT in the UK. Ian Graham brought Thought Field Therapy (TFT) to the UK. He immediately formed the BTFTA to establish professional guidelines and recognition. Both Robin and Ian are founding members in the professional organization which has paved the way for TFT's acceptance in mainstream health care, and, provided support and guidance to most UK practitioners.

They are both long time trainers of TFT Algorithm level courses so are in a unique position to understand the challenges that new practitioners will face and how best to resolve them. This guide clearly demonstrates their vast knowledge, experience and high degree of professionalism.

We have always been proud to have them represent TFT in the UK, knowing they did so with passion and integrity, even in the face of adversity. Ian's scholarly works and writings have supported TFT through many difficult tests for over a decade.

This guide provides a clear path of application, troubleshooting and practice guidelines for any new TFT practitioner. It also is great support for any existing practitioner, as their carefully selected case studies and evaluations are an invaluable resource for others in clinical application.

They have done an excellent job of developing an awareness of TFT in the UK and building a professional organization to support TFT practitioners. We are proud to have them as leaders and representatives for TFT in the United Kingdom.

Roger J. Callahan, PhD
Founder and Developer of Thought Field Therapy
Chairman of the Board, Association for Thought Field Therapy
Joanne M. Callahan, MBA
President, Callahan Techniques, Ltd.
President, ATFT Foundation
Treasurer, Association for Thought Field Therapy

Introduction

I have written this book together with the invaluable input of my colleague, Ian Graham, who brought Thought Field Therapy to this country in 1996 from America. It is an in-depth practical guide to assist everyone in their usage of TFT, including those who maybe experiencing difficulties with their practice due to initial inexperience or lack of confidence, and need instant assistance.

This need has become apparent through my experience of ten years of teaching Callahan Techniques Thought Field Therapy Algorithms to a wide variety of students and learning of their precise needs when faced with the practical requirements for administering TFT treatments to their clients. These needs have been shown not only from the many questions received during training, but also from the case studies sent to me after training for my constructive feedback.

It is also written for the many practitioners, both complementary and orthodox, who have maybe heard of 'the tapping technique' but know nothing about it and are inclined to dismiss it as a weird practice which is not worthy of their attention.

I would invite all of you to read this book because it will show you how Thought Field Therapy, created by the eminent psychologist Dr. Roger Callahan, is based on the reality of fact born out of experience of treatments given over the last thirty years all over the world.

Thought Field Therapy is a major psychological advance for professional practitioners to use *within* their particular discipline. Although it can well be used as a standalone technique, many professionals have found it to be an incredibly valuable addition to their therapeutic toolbox. There have been many psychologists and counsellors who have told me after their training that they find TFT speeds up and greatly assists in their work. They have discovered how its early use rapidly resolves many core issues so that subsequent cognitive work has far greater effect in clearing the total problem.

So "Thought Field Therapy - The Definitive Guide for Successful Practice" is for:

- everyone who is new to TFT and the use of Energy Psychology in general.

- those of you who have been trained some time ago but have not used the therapy very much, now feel you would really like to bring it into your work, but are finding yourself a bit rusty!

- those who are well practised but sometimes need extra assistance to cope with a complex problem that can leave you wondering where to start with TFT.

- for all Complementary Therapists who work with the body's meridian system within any discipline. These treatments can sometimes trigger the buried memory of a past trauma or fear. With TFT at your finger tips the sudden eruption of emotional distress can be released in minutes.

"Thought Field Therapy - The Definitive Guide for Successful Practice" is something which can address your immediate needs in a quick and informative way so that you can continue with what you were doing with minimum delay, knowing you can always go back later for more detail. Most importantly you will receive fast help for the particular difficulty you face.

Your training manual and book gave you the full account of how and why TFT works, exactly how you should do it for perfect results and some guidance about what to do if TFT is not working. But these are probably not able to give the precise information you need to cope with a more unusual or complex problem. Ideally, you need the support I give when trainees contact me and say , *"Robin, I've got this client who is coming next Thursday with this, that, or the other problem - how do I tackle it? "*

There are various ways to use this book:

- as a professional practitioner's handbook to locate specific information or to obtain some needed revision.

- as a form of interesting validation by concentrating on the case examples and studies which all describe real life treatments. Those that are case studies from students are designed to be instructive since they will highlight mistakes made (or perhaps a clumsy use of our therapy!), with suggestions of improvement for future use.

- You can read it from cover to cover! I hope you enjoy the narrative and the information it gives you.

As a TFT Handbook you will first find your way to the subject you require by the chapter heading in the front contents index. Then the first page of the chapter will list particular aspects of the subject which are then numbered so that you can quickly turn to the part needed. At the end of the chapter you will find actual treatment examples and student case studies for further reading which will greatly add to your understanding, knowledge and efficiency.

1. The TFT Protocol

1. Algorithms
2. The TFT Architecture
3. Using the SUD scale effectively
4. How to give a TFT Treatment
5. Further Ideas
6. The Protocol Summery
7. Case Studies from students

One of the most important parts of your training to become a capable TFT practitioner is, without doubt, your full understanding of the TFT Protocol. It is not intended to make life difficult for you or interfere with your freedom to get on with the job!

The protocol is needed to set your feet on a path which leads as quickly and efficiently as possible to your goal of total resolution of your client's problem. Without this help, I can almost guarantee you will quickly get into a muddle.

For example: *"I've done the majors but nothing's happened, so I'll try a PR correction. Oh dear! That hasn't helped - lets try another PR correction. Now what! ? That hasn't helped either! Oh dear, this doesn't seem to be going very well. I know, I'll repeat the whole algorithm and it'll probably work all right this time. Oh no! That made no difference and I believe my client is beginning to get fed up. OH HELP! ! "*

Well, at least there's one good result to be found from our poor practitioner's total mess! Apart from any frustration for the client, he has done no harm to the person!

To cut a long story short, the protocol is literally a step-by-step guide to pilot you through the needs of various PR corrections in the proper order as well as other actions needed to attain a satisfactory solution. Because of my past experience in helping many TFT students over the years to follow the TFT protocol exactly as intended, I make no apologies for taking you right back to the beginning - a very good place to start!

1. Algorithms.

You are using algorithms to treat your clients' problems. An algorithm is a set sequence of tapping points on the body used to address a specific problem. These sequences were discovered by Dr. Roger Callahan during the '80s and early '90s using his causal diagnostic methods. The sequences were confirmed over a period of years by diagnostic practitioners in many countries throughout the world continually finding the same sequence for each particular problem.

When Roger Callahan found these sequences were coming up through diagnosis eight times out of ten, he would then declare the sequence to be an algorithm. This is why we know the algorithms will succeed for 80% of your clients. This is why we know *you will* - not may - have an 80% success rate in resolving your clients' problems!

Thought Field Therapy

However this success depends entirely on following the TFT protocol accurately and faithfully!

2. The TFT Architecture

All algorithms follow the same pattern. It is vital that you complete each step in exactly the order shown to obtain efficient and reliable success.

Here is a typical example for an Anxiety/Fear Algorithm written out using our standard abbreviations:

e - a - c - 9g - sq

e, a and c are all tapping points,[1] each called a major

e - a - c is the sequence of the 3 majors which must be tapped in that order for this algorithm

9 g is the 9 Gamut sequence which must be performed next.

sq means "repeat the first sequence of majors"

The complete treatment is known as a **Holon**. Written out in full it would be:

e - a - c	9g	e - a - c
Tap these majors in this order	Do the whole 9 gamut sequence	Tap these majors again

Now Stop!

---

[1] Meridian Tapping Points and 9 gamut sequence - see Appendix 1

Every algorithm consists only of three main parts as shown in this Holon.

So you need to: Tap the Majors - do the 9 Gamut - Tap the same Majors - and stop!

Please do not award me with another 9 Gamut after the repeat of Majors or worse, an extra 9g followed by more Majors and a PR correction thrown in for good measure! Yes - these things have happened!

Always remember that TFT is very precise. It always follows a defined plan which gives great efficiency and speed of treatment. If you find the process going haywire then you know the protocol has been (temporarily!) lost.

3. Using the SUD scale effectively

One of the most common observations that new clients make about any previous conventional therapy experience is that their therapist *"didn't seem to listen to me"*. When asked to elaborate, the problem usually boils down to the fact that the therapist was regularly telling the client how they felt, not the other way round. *"You're doing so much better this week"*, the client would be told - and two things would then happen...

The client would become confused because perhaps they **didn't** actually feel any better at all, and when asked by the therapist, *"Do you agree?"*, the client would answer "Yes" - when an authoritative figure asks you a question like that the answer had better be yes, of course!

OK, the above is a generalisation - it doesn't *always* happen like that - but why does it occur at all? The answer lies in **objective** testing - questions and tick boxes on sheets of paper for clients to complete, the final score being a measure of how the client feels.

Objective testing is very useful, it can be a good guide to client progress, free of observer bias and easily quantifiable, but paper-and-pencil tests should never take the place of a the simple subjective question, ***"How do you feel right now?"***

Furthermore, the field of psychotherapy had, until now, seldom enjoyed the phenomenon of a complete **cure**, that is, a client totally free of symptoms. Hence the ***degree*** of improvement was all important in assessing progress - objective testing needed once again.

However, with TFT we can now achieve complete cure and so objective testing of progress is of much less importance. We can now trust the client's subjective report of how they feel with great reliability, the target being a report of ***"no further problem whatsoever"***.

The therapist's assessment is largely taken out of the equation - he or she no longer tells the client how they are doing. No therapist report - no observer bias - no confirmation bias. It is down to the client and the client alone to confirm whether or not the therapy has worked.

The single most important and powerful measurement tool we have in TFT is the ***client's report of their own experience.***

Objective testing tries to eliminate the possibility that the client may be misreporting his or her true emotional state. But do we need to be concerned that the client may be covering up his or her actual feelings by misreporting a value? Not at all - what we're looking for is the absolute endpoint - the complete absence of symptoms. Would a client actually misreport that significant event?

So, the way we measure this is through the use of the **Subjective Units of Distress (SUD) Scale**, (developed by cognitive-behavioural therapist, Joseph Wolpe, in 1969) where the client is asked to rate their level of discomfort on a 10 point (1-10) or 11 point (0-10) scale.[2]

---

[2] Whilst the 10 or 11 point scale is the most common way of obtaining a self-reported measure, *any* scale or description with point by point changes is acceptable as long as the client is able to be consistent in their report. The key factor is that the scale must have a definite "no further distress" endpoint.

Thought Field Therapy

Wolpe's SUD scale went something like this:

SUD	Subjective Experience
10	Feeling unbearably bad, out of control, as in a nervous breakdown, overwhelmed. The subject may feel so upset that he does not want to talk because he cannot imagine how anyone could possibly understand his agitation.
9	Feeling desperate, or very, very bad; losing control of emotions which are almost unbearable. The subject may be afraid of what he might do.
8	The beginning of alienation, approaching loss of control.
7	On the edge of some definitely bad feelings, maintains control with difficulty.
6	Feeling bad to the point that subject begins to think something ought to be done about the way he feels.
5	Moderately upset, uncomfortable. Unpleasant feelings are still manageable with some effort.
4	Somewhat upset, to the point that the subject cannot easily ignore an unpleasant thought; feeling uncomfortable.
3	Mildly upset, worried, bothered to the point that the subject notices it.
2	A little bit upset, but not noticeable unless the subject pays attention to his feelings and then realises there is something bothering him.
1	No acute distress and feeling basically good, if the subject makes special effort he might feel something unpleasant, but not much.
0	Peace, serenity, total relief, no bad feelings of any kind about any particular issue, even after special effort to feel unpleasant.

It really does not matter how your client defines their own SUD scale provided that the final value of 1 or 0, depending on the scale range you use, is understood **very clearly**.

It is also important to emphasise to clients they should give you a number that represents ***how they are feeling right at that very moment,*** just thinking about the problem, ***not*** how they have felt in the past or how they anticipate they might feel in the future.

A useful approach is to use this sentence once you have the client thinking about their specific problem: *"On a scale of zero to ten, with 10 being the worst and zero being "no bad feelings at all", tell me how you feel right now - not how it **has been** in the past nor how it **might be** in the future, but **right now**, as you speak to me"*

Now make sure you write it down and confirm *again* that the score given is how the client is feeling right now. After successful treatment, clients sometimes deny that they really meant the score that they originally gave, so it's essential that you do labour this point.

Progress is judged by asking for the SUD at very specific points in the treatment. It is also very important to remind the client to focus ***only*** on the problem / feeling / emotion / etc. that they thought about when they ***originally*** gave their SUD.

You should also bear in mind that a client who represses their feelings (usually as a coping mechanism in chronic conditions) will not be able to give you a SUD. Such a client will not get upset when asked simply to think about the problem, but may actually have to be exposed to the triggering factor.

Thought Field Therapy

Don't worry! This inability to give a SUD will ***not interfere with the effectiveness of the treatment in any way.*** There will still be a treatable thought field simply because they are thinking of their problem. The only difficulty lies in not getting immediate feedback on whether or not the treatment you provided worked or not.

In such a case, administer the algorithm, following all the steps outlined in the protocol, with the exception of asking for a SUD. Since you won't know in this case whether or not the client is reversed, it is a good idea also to treat for all levels of reversal in advance of the treatment.

After treatment, you will need to ask the client to test the treatment out in a real life situation, ***as soon as possible*** (toxin exposure may undo the successful treatment) and report back to you on whether or not there has been a change.

Using the SUD with Children

When working with children, make sure that they are in the thought field before treating them. This is quite easy with children who have learned to talk, of course! You might use words or pictures to obtain the thought. You could ask the child to draw a picture themselves that shows the problem.

However, you achieve this, as soon as the child is in the thought field, administer the treatment.

If the child does not wish to remember the event or problem in any way, you could also resort to simple psychology - advise the child **not** to think about it!

Of course, trying ***not*** to think about something immediately means that one has to think about that very thing! The thought field will be present and you can commence treatment. During the process you can easily reinforce the thought field by saying *"You're not thinking about (the problem), are you?"*

If a child is responsive but has not yet learned to talk, you could show pictures related to the problem or expose the child to the problem situation. In this case we're dealing with a **perceptual field**, a thought field by any other name.

If you're treating a baby, you could hold or touch the baby and tap on yourself as a surrogate. Since you are essentially merging body fields with the baby, the treatment will still work. You could also tap or rub the points on the baby's body, with the express permission of the child's parents, of course. Clearly, the baby will be unable to perform actions required in the 9 gamut sequence so it can be performed by the therapist or parent whilst in bodily contact with the baby.

With older children, one can obtain a useable SUD by having them show with hands apart (in much the same way as a fisherman would demonstrate the size of a fish) how big their "bad feelings" are.

You could also provide objects such as marbles on a dish - the more marbles the child keeps on the dish the worse they feel. Ask them to take as many marbles off the dish as they wish as the treatment progresses.

Alternatively, have them point to a chart like the one that follows:.

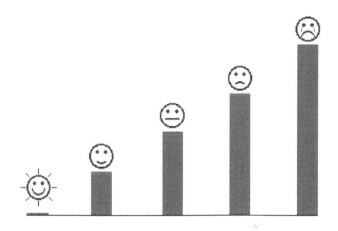

If a parent or guardian is present you can also ask if they notice any change in the child's behaviour after the treatment.

Let's emphasise again - the SUD scale can be anything you want it to be provided that the maximum and minimum values are understood and agreed by both therapist and client.

4. How to give a TFT Treatment

Let us assume your client has just arrived for treatment using TFT. Now - it's fine to work with both of you standing up - TFT will work perfectly well - could be useful if it's a rush job! However, most people prefer to sit down and I suggest sitting opposite and reasonably close to your client so that he will find it very simple to copy your actions while you tap on yourself. And yes - this will cause you to receive the treatment also!

This is no bad thing - if you don't share the problem, nothing will happen. If you do share the problem, you'll receive the benefit too! It also prevents you taking on board the client's problem, a major hazard in conventional psychotherapy.

Your first step should be to give a quick explanation of how TFT works because most people have (so far!) never heard of the technique and for some this is a cause for concern and you need to reassure your person as quickly as possible.

I mention a case in the Traumatic Stress chapter where I helped a young woman who had recently lost her child. She was so very anxious as she feared that TFT treatment might totally remove her memory of the child!

This was very definitely a case where it was necessary to spend some time explaining how TFT is able to remove great distress whilst leaving her treasured memory untouched. Or rather, *improved* - since she was now able to remember details that had previously been denied to her by her upsetting emotion. To have started treatment before being satisfied that she was totally reassured would have been cruel.

For most people a quick explanation as to why your treatment is very different to traditional psychotherapy is all that's needed. Nevertheless, sometimes you will have a client with a very enquiring mind who will want to know a great deal of how and why TFT can work.

Very often the sheer speed of the treatment is virtually unacceptable to such people because it flies in the face of long established psychological practice that has been used over generations - and is still being used!

Thought Field Therapy

This will inevitably lead to much apex explanation after treatment and, coming often from an intelligent mind, the client's response will be worth remembering to add to your collection!

Here is a nice little thought sequence that may help your sceptical clients:

Psychological problems arise in thoughts and their subsequent responses.

Thoughts have no mass - so no inertia.

An e-mail has no mass - no inertia

An e-mail will arrive in Australia in a few seconds. **We expect this**

Equally, an upsetting thought can go in a few seconds. **We don't expect this!**

So, having explained and if necessary reassured your client about this strange treatment called Thought Field Therapy, your next vital task is to find out exactly how you can help your client. Easily said but not easily done!

To explore this most important part of your treatment in depth, please go to Chapter 3 - 'Finding the Problem Thought Fields.'

It is no exaggeration to say that the vast majority of your successes will come from knowing how to question your client about his problem and so identify the thought fields that need treatment.

Suffice it to say at this point, you need to talk with your client about their problem(s) in depth - and be aware that while you need to find out about core issues, the client will busily tell you all about what is immediately of his concern. Don't be tempted to rush in and treat these since they are often driven by the core issues that must be addressed first.

I know you're probably thinking: *"but TFT is not a talk therapy"* - and you are quite right. This initial discussion is not therapy but rather a 'diagnostic tool' to discover exactly what needs treatment. Then we get down to using the TFT technique now that the client is only **thinking** of the problem. Always remember with TFT that it's what the person is **thinking about** that is treated.

Some years ago, I had a visit from a middle aged lady who had a collection of problems, so I started to talk to her about these problems - or perhaps more accurately, she told me - at length.

It quickly became obvious that she was really keen to tell me every minute detail! From time to time I tried to ask a question or put in a comment, but her continuous flow was quite unstoppable! It seemed that nothing would slow her down in order that I could ask for the information I needed!

In the end, after literally half an hour, I said in a firm voice: *"Please will you stop talking otherwise I cannot treat you! "* Fortunately she got the message with no offence and we were able to make some progress. This was an extreme case!

So, having discovered from discussion with your client exactly the thought field that needs to be addressed, decide on the correct algorithm required and start your treatment:

EXAMPLE 1.

Ask Client to Think about Problem. Get initial SUD (e.g. 10) Write it down!

This seems obvious and simple enough but has several pit-falls! First you should tell your client that you need to know how much upset thinking of the problem is causing right **now**.

Once again - not how bad it was at the time, or yesterday or how bad the client knows it will be later today - but specifically: *'How much upset is the thought causing you now, at this moment?'* Sometimes this clarification will suddenly 'get through' and you will be aware that 'the machinery' in the person's head is activated and he will say: *"Oh! You mean now?"* and then immediately give you a lower SUD which is the true figure you need. This true figure is important because it will accurately relate to the further SUDs you will obtain during the treatment which reflect how the degree of upset is progressing - thus giving the guide you need.

Another difficulty can be for those who present with multiple disorders such as complex anxieties and fears. From the TFT point of view this means the client has a 'basketful' of thought fields, each one causing a particular anxiety/fear.

You need your person to be thinking about just one of these thought fields because you cannot treat a whole basketful at once! But because these thought fields are usually closely associated to the total problem, your client will have the habit of thinking of the whole lot at once as 'my problem'. Therefore you need to spend a little time carefully explaining why it's essential to think **only** of one particular aspect (thought field) of the problem and then continually check that **only this aspect** is actually being kept in mind.

The process is often referred to as the 'onion layer' principle. The first treatment should be for the part of the problem that causes your client the greatest amount of upset now. Having cleared this, move on to the next most upsetting aspect - the next 'onion layer.' Continue in this way - maybe over a few sessions - until all 'layers' have been resolved, remembering that until the last layer has been treated your client will not report that the problem has gone. In other words, the onion, having had its layers removed will be smaller - but it will still be 'an onion'!

As a consequence of the Apex experience whereby people have great difficulty in believing that TFT has had any effect on their problem, it is common for your client to deny that the initial SUD given immediately before starting treatment *"was really that high,"*

It's therefore wise **always** to write the initial SUD down when it's given to you so that you can literally prove it was the case! Even then it's quite possible the person will not really believe you - but at least it helps!

Tap the Majors Get a SUD (e.g. 9)

Tap on yourself at the same time, so that your client can easily copy you and then ask for the SUD. Your next action depends entirely on this SUD report. Remembering that in a successful TFT treatment, the SUD **always** falls in quantum leaps, anything less than a 2-point drop is automatically suspect and you **must not allow yourself to continue with the next part of the algorithm.**

Thought Field Therapy

In this example the initial SUD was 10 and the reply to your enquiry: *"How do you feel now? "* may well receive the answer: *"Yes, that's a little better." "How much better, please give me a number." "Oh, it's 9 now."*

This is unreliable and is more likely to be your client trying to please you! Just to prove the point, I usually gently challenge this report by saying: *"It hasn't really changed has it? "* - to which the reply is almost always to agree with you: *"No it hasn't really."*

So you're still at SUD 10. What do you do now?

Remember that there will always be a reason for anything not happening as expected. You are now looking for the reason so it can be put right and you can continue on your merry way! So you are essentially looking for a block to your progress and the most likely reason is Psychological Reversal. [3]

Treat for Specific PR

While demonstrating on yourself, have your client tap the side of hand PR spot about 20 times **while thinking about the problem**. **Do not** now ask again for the SUD! It will not have changed! Remember the PR treatment is used to remove the PR block to your progress. It will 'clear the way' so that the next time you carry out the treatment you will have success. Therefore, now go back to the beginning of the algorithm and:

Repeat the Majors Get a SUD (e.g. 7)

After every PR correction, no matter of what type or where it occurs in the algorithm, **always go right back**

---
[3] Psychological Reversal PR – see Chapter 2

to the beginning and start again. This is **not** the same as repeating the algorithm.

Never - repeat never - be tempted to try running through the algorithm again without first correcting for PR. If it did not work the first time, it will not work the second or third, or hundredth, time and you will have a frustrated client who will walk out on you and tell everyone how useless TFT was for him! Not good for your reputation or for any TFT practitioner!

If on the other hand you have just used a PR correction to remove the block to progress, when you then repeat the majors you are now working in a new space which effectively means you are doing the majors for the first time. So having repeated the majors you now again ask for the SUD. In this example the initial SUD was 10 which really did not move. Now the client reports SUD 7. This shows your PR correction has worked and immediately your client feels an improvement.

As you have now obtained the minimum acceptable 2-point drop in SUD, you are clear to progress to the next part of the algorithm and:

Do the 9 Gamut Sequence, Get a SUD (e.g. 4)

This is the middle part of the algorithm and is always done in its entirety. Start by showing your client the gamut spot (demonstrating on yourself, as always) and start him continuously tapping. Very often this leads the person to look down at what is being done in order to concentrate on the job in hand!

Since this position will be useless for the 9g process, ask the person to hold his head up and look at you and

Thought Field Therapy

remind him to continue with the tapping. Then ask for eyes open and eyes shut.

Now use your hands and arms to indicate glancing down one side and then the other side while instructing not to move the head. Do the same thing to show rolling eyes in a circular movement one way and the opposite way. **But watch out!** I promise you this is where your client is so busy thinking about eye movement that the gamut tapping will stop! Do a quick reminder: *"Keep tapping"* and watch out for it possibly happening again.

Now with the final part of 9g be sure that the client is really humming. This is important since creating only pure music, humming will largely involve the right hemisphere of the brain which is what we want. Some people will happily give you 'La La La or Ha Ha Ha' but as these are words they will largely activate the speech centre located in the left hemisphere.

Finally on completion of the whole 9g sequence, please remember to tell your client to **stop tapping!** Having got the person going in the first place, you will now find he won't stop!

So, having completed the second part of the algorithm, remind him to think about the problem and give you the present SUD. Now, let's say the report is a SUD of 4 So this again shows we have the required minimum 2-point drop (7 down to 4) and therefore you can allow yourself to go ahead with the final part of the algorithm:

Repeat the Majors Get a SUD (e.g. 2)

After tapping the majors the report this time is a 2. Assuming we're working on a 1 to 10 scale, it's now a good idea to ask the client: *"Has the problem very nearly gone?"* and if the reply is *"Yes it has but I think there is still just something there"* - then you can be sure the person is genuinely down to a 2 and not still at SUD 3 or 4. Being SUD 2 or less you can now apply our good friend and...

Finish with the Floor-to-Ceiling Eye-Roll [4] which, virtually without fail, will bring a SUD of 2 down to 1. Be aware that it does not work for a SUD above 2! Confirm this by now asking the client: *"How does the problem feel now?"* If the answer is: *"Now it has gone, it's completely gone"* you know that your treatment is complete.

If after the final majors the SUD was immediately down to 1, still use the eye roll to put a seal or finish to the process. You have now completed an excellent TFT treatment and you should have a grateful client who is probably apexing like mad!

EXAMPLE 2.

Ask Client to Think about Problem. Get initial SUD (e.g. 10) Write it down!

From now on I'm assuming you are following my advice as given in the first example to ensure you receive a correct SUD for the start of your treatment.

Tap the Majors Get a SUD (e.g. 2)

Wait a minute! What's happening here? SUD now only **2**? ! But we've only tapped the majors - has something gone wrong? !

No nothing is wrong - and for a new student to TFT who has never experienced this, I promise it will happen to you sooner or later! Really, we should not be too surprised.

[4.] Floor-to-Ceiling Eye-Roll er - see Appendix 1

Thought Field Therapy

When we remember Dr. Callahan's experience with Mary all those years ago when he simply asked her to tap under her eye, not only was the treatment using only the one major (under the eye) but her SUD (if one had been given) would have come rushing down from a 10 to 1.

So what do you do now? You haven't done the 9 gamut nor the repeat of majors to complete the algorithm! Please don't do them just because they're there. You're already down to a SUD 2 and so they're not needed. Simply enlist the services of our good friend and...

Finish with the Eye-Roll

This will bring the SUD 2 down to 1. Finally check with the client that all traces of the problem have now gone.

Remember the eye roll is also an excellent treatment used on its own as a Rapid Relaxation Exercise. So whenever you are feeling a little tense and un-relaxed - just do an eye roll - and feel better!

EXAMPLE 3.

Ask Client to Think about Problem. Get initial SUD (e.g. 9) Write it down!

Tap the Majors Get a SUD (e.g. 9)

So here we have a block to progress and must:

Treat for Specific PR

Tap the side of hand PR spot about 20 times **whilst thinking about the problem**.

Repeat the Majors Get a SUD (e.g. 9)

So our progress is still blocked and so we must now:

Treat for Recurring PR

After showing your client how to find the Sore Spot on the **left** side of chest, have him copy you while you gently rub your spot in a circular motion about ten times **whilst thinking about the problem**.

Repeat the Majors Get a SUD (e.g. 7)

That's better - we have some movement! Since the SUD has fallen the minimum 2-point drop necessary for progress, we can now allow ourselves to move on and:

Do the 9 Gamut Sequence Get a SUD (e.g. 4)

Again the drop in SUD is enough to move on to:

Repeat the Majors Get a SUD (e.g. 2)

This is fine so:

Finish with the Eye-Roll

This will bring the SUD 2 down to 1. Finally check with the client that all traces of the problem have now gone.

<u>EXAMPLE 4.</u>

Ask Client to Think about Problem. Get initial SUD (e.g. 8) Write it down!

Tap the Majors Get a SUD (e.g. 7)

We know this is a false report and so we have a block to progress and must:

Treat for Specific PR

Tap the side of hand PR spot about 20 times **while thinking about the problem**.

Thought Field Therapy

Repeat the Majors Get a SUD (e.g. 5)

This is fine so:

Do the 9 Gamut Sequence Get a SUD (e.g. 4)

Since we have already resolved half the person's upset, we are now looking at a block to **what remains** of the problem. Therefore it's necessary to:

Treat for Mini PR

Tap the side of hand PR spot about 5 or 6 times **whilst thinking about what REMAINS of the problem.**

Repeat the Majors Get a SUD (e.g. 1)

Remember after every PR correction, no matter where it occurs in the algorithm, **always go right back to the beginning and start again**. In this case it can potentially leave you with the whole of the algorithm to repeat from start to finish. However it is usual for the repeat of majors only to be all that's needed as shown here. Finally, as always:

Finish with the Eye-Roll

Check that SUD is still 1 and client is not aware of any upset at all.

EXAMPLE 5.

Ask Client to Think about Problem. Get initial SUD (e.g. 9) Write it down!

Tap the Majors Get a SUD (e.g. 9)

No progress so:

Treat for Specific PR

Tap the side of hand PR spot about 5 or 6 times **whilst thinking about the problem**.

Repeat the Majors Get a SUD (e.g. 9)

Still no progress so:

Treat for Recurring PR

Rub Sore spot on **left** side of chest **whilst thinking of the problem**.

Repeat the Majors Get a SUD (e.g. 9)

Still no progress so go for the next PR in line which is:

Treat for Massive PR

Rub Sore Spot on left chest **whilst thinking of limitations and problems in general**.

Repeat the Majors Get a SUD (e.g. 9)

It is now becoming apparent that there is a problem which may not be due only to PR. But it's worth one more attempt so:

Treat for Level 2 PR

Tap under nose about 5 or 6 times **whilst thinking about the problem**.

Repeat the Majors Get a SUD (e.g. 9)

So even a Level 2 PR correction is not helping in this case and so we must look for a completely different reason for the block to treatment.

Thought Field Therapy

5. Further Ideas

If you've got this far it will be obvious you're 'flogging a dead horse' and so it's essential you look for other reasons that might be blocking your progress. Your next best step therefore is to:

Treat with Collarbone Breathing (cb²)

Remember that Collarbone Breathing[5] is a specific treatment to address a state of Neurological Disorganisation. As with the 9-gamut treatment, cb^2 is always done in its entirety remembering to remind your client to 'keep tapping the gamut spot'. It is quite usual for a person who has several associated problems leading, for example to depressive feelings, to be suffering also from neurological disorganisation. As always, ensure your client is **thinking about the problem**.

Get a SUD (e.g. 7)

Yes I know - we haven't repeated the majors first! This is because cb^2 is different. It is **not** a variation on PR treatment since it does not address PR. As such it will often solve a problem for you and will always, when successful, bring the SUD down two or more points. **Now** go back to the beginning of your algorithm, repeat the majors and this time you will almost certainly obtain a further drop in the SUD and you can happily continue from that point!

Check client's thinking

Another major reason for your lack of progress which has nothing to do with PR can be due to your client's thinking.

[5.] Collarbone Breathing Exercise see Appendix 2

Remember as I've said before : 'It is what your client is thinking about that gets treated.' So if he is thinking about a collection of thought fields which put together form 'my problem', you are not going to make any progress because you cannot treat half-a-dozen thought fields at once. So check at an early stage that your person is truly **only thinking** about the particular problem you had agreed on before the start of your treatment. If this produces a sudden and obvious change in thinking, go back to the beginning and:

Tap the Majors Get a SUD (e.g. 6)

Now you're under way and can continue with the rest of the holon.

Next we must consider Toxins.

Toxins can be literally anything a person eats, drinks or inhales to which they have a **sensitivity** (not necessarily an allergy), and they can either completely block treatment in the first place, or later undo a successful treatment at any time after its completion - days, months, or years later. As the diagnosis and treatment of toxins is a major subject on its own, we shall not take it further at this stage.

For the purposes of giving a TFT treatment, if you are finding yourself getting stuck as in this final example, do think about toxins being the cause. It is not unusual for your client to be sitting in front of you busily breathing in a toxin! For example, did the lady you are seeing literally waft her way into the room leaving a trail of perfume behind her!? Women are frequently toxic to their perfume.

Then there are many other inhalant possibilities for men and women. Hair Spray, Shampoo, Moisturiser and all make-up, Men's Cologne, Deodorant, Body Lotion and Clothing - or more often the Washing Powder / Fabric Conditioner they were last washed in.

If you suspect any of these as a possible **inhalant** toxin for your client, then having identified the particular culprit, have your client think about the toxin and tap the Index Finger 20 times followed by the Side of Hand PR Spot. This will often clear the effect of the toxin for a while and so give you a 'window of opportunity' to resolve the problem.

Get a SUD

Here again we are not dealing with a PR correction which will clear the way so that your next treatment - repeat of majors - will be effective. This is an actual treatment which temporarily negates the effect of the inhalant toxin and so immediately you can expect the SUD to reduce if the treatment is successful. Then:

Tap the Majors Get a SUD

Now you're under way and should progress to total resolution of your client's problem without any further trouble.

6. The Protocol Summary

The basic TFT process is to administer a complete Algorithm while treating for any PR or other blocks to progress along the way.

The Holon is made up from three parts: Majors - 9 Gamut - Majors. No more!

Ask for the SUD after each part and **never** allow yourself to progress to the next part of the Holon unless you have a **minimum drop of 2 points**.

<u>If no minimum drop in SUD after the Majors</u>:

First try **Specific PR** correction - Tap Side of Hand PR Spot while thinking of problem.

Next try **Recurring PR** correction - Rub Sore Spot while thinking of problem.

Next try **Massive PR** correction - Rub Sore Spot while thinking of problems in general

Remember **Mini PR** correction - Tap Side of Hand PR Spot while thinking of what **remains** of problem. (Occurs late in treatment).

Further try **Level 2 PR** correction - Tap Under Nose while thinking of problem.

Great help **Collarbone Breathing** - Administer complete treatment while thinking of problem. Get immediate SUD Continue with Algorithm.

Check **Client's Thinking** - Ensure properly tuned into desired Thought Field. Continue with Algorithm.

Suspect **Toxins** - Inhalant toxins - Tap Index Finger 20 times & Side of Hand PR Spot while thinking of toxin. Get immediate SUD Continue with Algorithm.

Finally, remember:

The first two or three PR corrections should be used initially in the order shown. After that, use any other

Thought Field Therapy

correction or treatment as shown to be needed by information from the client and/or your intuition which will increase with practise!

The golden rule of never progressing with treatment without the minimum drop of 2 points of SUD will only apply to SUDS of 6 and up. This is because at the lower levels we cannot always expect 2-point drops since the SUD does not have far enough to go! Therefore one-point progress at the lower levels would be acceptable.

Last, but most certainly not least, if you have a problem where you really are completely stuck and simply do not know what to do next, **STOP!** Don't be tempted in desperation and without logical thinking to 'have another go at this' or 'perhaps try a bit more of that'! This will certainly not help and will probably upset your client.

Equally please do not send your client away with apologies for not being able to help with his problem. Remember there is always someone else who works at the Diagnostic or VT level who will be able to help.

So, please, always, refer these clients as it would be very unfair to deny them the chance of successful treatment just because you are not (yet) able to heal them yourself. Trust me, this will not happen often since the Algorithms are extremely effective and you will enjoy many successes!

7. Case study from student

(a). Case Study from student: 'Trauma or Anxiety? '

A woman 31 years old was in a serious road accident which has led to her being disabled and now has to use crutches to help herself get around.

She has feelings of anxiety when she goes to bed, clenches her teeth and feels her hands grasping on her body which leaves marks on her arms. Very tense as she thinks she is disturbing her partner, snoring, grinding her teeth and this causes her to worry and so she does not get a good night's sleep. When her partner gets up in the morning she feels able to relax.

Used algorithm for anxiety/stress:

Initial SUD 10 After 1st Majors: SUD 10

PR correction and repeated 1st Majors: SUD 4

9-gamut and 2nd Majors - did sequence once more and anxiety went to SUD 1

Completed with eye-roll.

She felt her jaw drop after SUD 4 and became more relaxed and felt less anxious.

Continued treatment as she had pain.

Used algorithm for physical pain:

Initial SUD 10 After 1st Majors: SUD 7

After 9-gamut: SUD 7 PR

Changed to alternative algorithm for physical pain as I thought she may respond better to this one:

Thought Field Therapy

SUD 7 After 1st Majors: SUD 3

9-gamut finished sequence: SUD 1 Finished with eye-roll.

Client felt she had only an ache to her lower back and to her jaw. Apparently she is always massaging her jaw.

My reply:

Certainly a good result using both Anxiety/Fear algorithm and then the Pain algorithm. However I don't think you have really got to the root of her problem. The serious road accident which has even left her with a permanent disability would be a major trauma for her. The teeth clenching and body grasping would be part of her PTSD. I'm sure, if you ask her, the actual accident will be continually replaying in her head. This is the core issue which is driving all her present anxieties and fears and possibly also helping to cause her pain.

So your first step should be to get her to think of being in the actual accident now and treat that with complex Trauma together with any anger or guilt that may also be present. Being the root cause of her problems, you will find that her anxieties will almost certainly have disappeared after the treatment and she will also be aware of a great weight being lifted which will lead to feeling calm and relaxed. As it is, you have removed her presenting anxiety problems but have left the actual cause untreated. Your treating the pain as you did was fine.

Initially your protocol seems to be a little muddled! Working with the anxiety/fear you did the PR correction after being stuck at SUD 10 and then repeated the majors - fine! Then you seem to have done the 9-gamut and the second majors and *'did the sequence once more? ? '*

Having progressed so well from 10 to 4 after the initial PR correction and repeat of majors, the next step is 9-gamut and again ask for the SUD. If it has now dropped to 2, finish with the eye-roll to bring it to 1. If down to 3, now use the final part of the algorithm - repeat the majors. (One point drop from 4 to 3 is all right at this low level of SUD because 4 cannot go very far since it's already low). Finally if the SUD was stuck at 4 after the 9-gamut, then correct with a Mini PR (PR to what *remains* of the problem) and then go back to the beginning and repeat the majors. (Remember you always go back to the beginning of the algorithm after any PR correction). In the event you managed to get there and finish with the eye-roll.

I see you decided to change algorithms for her pain half way through the first holon and that's fine as your hunch seemed to be correct and you quickly obtained a good result. If you could see her again, do address the initial trauma as she does need to be treated for this and be sure to look for several associated traumas as part of the total experience. Each one could represent a different thought field and you may need to treat each one before the total traumatic experience is completely resolved.

2. Psychological Reversal

1. What is Psychological Reversal?
2. Types of PR and their Correction

1. What is Psychological Reversal?

A full understanding of Psychological Reversal - PR, its implications and how to manage it correctly is completely essential to your success as a TFT practitioner.

Beware any temptation to ignore it or take it for granted!

Gary Emery PhD who is an expert on the cognitive treatment of anxiety and depression, has quoted: "Psychological Reversal is one of the most important discoveries in psychology"

As Dr. Callahan says in his book 'Stop the Nightmares of Trauma', PR is perhaps the most important fundamental concept for health, human progress, happiness and success that one may ever encounter.

It is easily treated but remember, if it were not for the discovery of PR our success rate of TFT would be reduced by around 50%. Many people for whom we now quickly resolve intense psychological problems would be completely untreatable if we were unable to correct psychological reversal.

PR is a state of reversed polarity in the body. In this condition your client will literally (but unconsciously) sabotage their own healing. Any healing - not just TFT! People will tend to do the opposite of what they are thinking of doing - typically, for example, an addict will continue to indulge in spite of really wanting to stop.

All of us are sometimes in a state of PR. It is worth explaining to your client that he will know how it feels at the end of a bad day when things have not been going well and he's feeling generally fed up, down and jaded! Your person will confirm knowing this state only too well! So explain: *"When you're feeling like this, the chances are you're in PR - so just tap the side of hand and you'll find it gives you a bit of lift and you'll feel better!"* Explain that it won't cure anything, but it will remove the PR and so you feel better. Also tell your client to teach it to his friends with the assurance that it can never do any harm but will usually give a little help.

In a different way, my wife, Mary, found she might need a quick PR treatment when she was being treated by a chiropractor. She realised that he was using kinesiology muscle testing to help his treatment so she tapped her side of hand to ensure he was not receiving incorrect results. As it happened, he was! He said *"What have you just done? Everything has changed!"* So she explained PR and its correction and suggested that he used it with his patients in future!

Thought Field Therapy

Recognising Psychological Reversal

- TFT or other treatments (e.g. a medical treatment that is normally effective) do not work.
- Reversing words, concepts and / or numbers.
- Dyslexia (likely to be a massive reversal state).
- Grumpy, irritable, negative mood.
- Self-sabotaging behaviour.
- Self-talk is very negative.
- Procrastination.
- Having a "mental block" in a particular area, such as mathematics, writing, computers, etc.
- Client does not respond to appropriate algorithm treatment but responds to same treatment after PR correction.

2. Types of PR and their Correction

Specific PR

This is the most usual form of PR and refers to the person being psychologically reversed specifically to a particular part of his life - typically the problem you are treating.

Correction: Tap PR Spot on side of hand about 10 times *while thinking of the problem*.

Recurring PR

This PR is one that will return quickly after correction and so needs a different treatment. Again it is specific to the problem being treated.

Correction: Rub the Sore Spot on the *left* side of chest about 10 times in a small circular movement ***while thinking of the problem***.

Why is the sore spot sore! ? It's believed to be linked to the location of the lymphatic system's thoracic duct, and any problem there is referred to that position on the skin.

When showing your client how to find the sore spot be certain to explain it's essential to press quite firmly with one finger whilst searching for it. It would be quite useless pussy-footing around giving gentle little pushes here and there! Having found the sore spot: *'Ow! - that one hurt'!* - then immediately urge your client to reduce the pressure while rubbing that spot more gently.

Here, also, we have an exception to the rule! TFT tapping points can be addressed on either side of the body. This side, that side or both sides at once - it doesn't matter.

But for the sore spot always go for the left side. Yes there is a sore spot on the right side but for most people it is harder to find and we don't want a desperate client leaving bruises!

Massive PR

We find this PR in people whose reversal affects most parts of their life. They often have a chronic bad mood and show a negative attitude to almost everything. This

Thought Field Therapy

reversal needs to be treated first if you are to have any chance of your TFT treatment working.

Correction: As for recurring PR, rub the Sore Spot on the left chest about 10 times - but *while thinking of problems and limitations in general.*

Mini PR

This little chap is so often misunderstood and yet is frequently needed as an important part of a successful treatment. As it's name implies we are dealing with a lesser or smaller PR because it occurs only when the client has already lost part of the problem but is now PR to the remainder. Typically a client has progressed to a SUD 4 after the 9-gamut but now shows no further improvement. This is because the person is now PR to *what remains of the problem.*

Correction: As for Specific PR, tap PR Spot on side of hand about 10 times *while thinking about what remains of the problem*.

Level 2 PR

Sometimes you will find that a Level 2 PR correction is needed after there is still no drop in SUD after trying all the above reversal corrections.

Correction: Tap Under Nose about 10 times *while thinking of the problem*.

Mini Level 2 PR

Not to be left out, there is also a mini version of Level 2 PR. This can be helpful where the SUD is stuck at a low value in spite of using corrections including Mini PR.

Correction: Tap Under Nose about 10 times *while thinking about **what remains** of the problem*.

3. Finding the Problem Thought Fields

1. Basic TFT principles
2. Finding the core issue
3. Looking for every thought field
4. Case studies

1. Basic TFT principles

Let us look back for a moment and review exactly what we are doing with TFT. Put simply, we are first identifying the thought field/s that contain perturbations which, being a locus of information, become active when the client thinks about his problem. This information is referred to the physical brain which in turn reacts to that information and so generates the emotional upset. You, as the practitioner, then use the body's meridian system to address and subsume the perturbations so that their information can no longer be passed to the brain and hence the upset is no longer experienced.

Remember the computer analogy: 'deleting the file' from the hard disc memory so that it is no longer possible to run the program called fear - or whatever - in inappropriate circumstances?

Also remember that as with the computer file, the perturbation is only removed from activity and does not disappear out of existence. Thus the 'computer guru' can retrieve the deleted file just as an exposure to a toxin can reactivate the perturbation in the thought field and the person is aware the problem has returned.

So, these are the simple 'mechanics' of TFT which in the absence of any complications take only minutes to resolve a client's problem. This speed is due to the fact that **TFT is simple!** It is because of this sheer speed and simplicity that so many in the traditional psychological and medical professions find it impossible to accept our therapy can be anything other than a 'quick fix'! However simplicity has long been praised and should not be confused with inadequacy.

Many professionals prefer things to be complicated - it might boost their ego to be seen working with something really complicated! Also something complicated should **not** be easy to treat! Sceptics will say that a simple treatment CANNOT work because it is too simple! These people should remember the wisdom of Albert Einstein:

'Keep it simple. As simple as possible. But no simpler.'

'If the idea is at first not absurd, then there is no hope for it.'

We should remember that the body will not transfer huge amounts of energy during healing if it can be avoided. It will always go for the route of lowest energy expenditure whenever possible and this is brilliantly given by using TFT. Even then you will notice that the amount of energy expended during many TFT treatments will often cause the client to feel a little weary after treatment - thus yawning is usually a sign of a successful outcome!

2. Finding the core issue

So, TFT is simple but it's people who are complicated! And this is what makes our therapy so fascinating. It is this very complication that makes a lie of the initial demand to: 'first get a brief statement of the problem (to identify the thought fields that contain perturbations to be addressed) and get an initial SUD.'

It will not be an exaggeration to suggest that at least 50-75% of your success in resolving clients' problems will be due to your ability to find the thought fields that need be treated.

I can hear you say: *"But that's obvious. My client says he's terrified of public speaking and so I just get him to think of standing up in front of a group of people and speaking to them, get an initial SUD and treat him with the fear algorithm = job well done! Simple! "* Well yes, in many 'simple' cases this may well be true. But is it really as simple as it first appears?

There are so many cases which at first glance will always appear to be vey simple usually because you are looking only at the presenting problems which are readily given to you by the client. If you go ahead and treat the presenting problems, TFT will usually produce a good result - for the time being. Almost certainly the problem will re-occur, often very soon, because you have not looked for the core issue which is the 'driving force' behind it.

In this case we need to ask: *"Do you know why you have this fear and how long have you suffered from it?"* Very often, for this the most common phobia, your client will only be able to say that he's suffered for as long as he can remember and can give no reason for it. It is interesting that this age old fear goes back in time when man first realised that snakes are one of the most effective, and so feared, of all land-based predators. This is shown most clearly by this phobia.

A while ago I was told by a woman who had a tremendous fear of public speaking that she once had no fear at all when speaking out in a hall full of people and she could not understand it! She explained that it was a political meeting in the local village hall and at one point she became so incensed with the speaker that she raised her voice and told him what she thought of his ideas! Although the hall was full of people, she had absolutely no fear (although at that point she might have needed treatment for anger!)

I asked where she was sitting in the hall and she explained that due to a traffic holdup she was late and had to squeeze in right at the back. This is exactly what I expected and I said: *"So you were speaking over the backs of everyone's head?"* *"Yes,* she confirmed, *but I could see the speaker on the platform quite clearly and I gave him what for!"* But she did not see the peoples' eyes as no-one would be looking at her while she was speaking.

Now think about the snake. What does it do immediately before striking its prey?

It fixes the animal with its eyes giving a straight penetrating stare. What normally happens to a person talking to a hall full of people? Everybody will be looking at the speaker and so for the phobic person there will be this great fear of so many eyes looking straight at him. There was once an experiment with blind people and they found none had any fear of public speaking!

So, let's go back again to our person terrified of speaking to a crowd or even just a few colleagues in a small group and ask: *"Do you know why you have this fear and how long you have suffered from it?"* This time he might well say: *"I never used to be afraid of speaking to any group of people and in fact used to enjoy giving the odd after-dinner speech. But now it's impossible - ever since that traumatic experience about ten years ago when I was threatened by.....and I haven't been able to give a speech since."* This would probably be something that happened when he was actually speaking and may well have involved several associated traumas and perhaps several people also.

This means you may find a complicated web of problems together causing traumatic fears which are now associated with any form of speaking in public. You treat with complex trauma but need to be certain by in-depth questioning that you find and treat all the associated thought fields that need to be resolved. Until this is done, you cannot be sure that the full core issue, which is driving his present fears, has been resolved.

So now we can see how our 'simple problem' can so easily not be simple at all. This means that it will always be your careful questioning that can show up the thought fields that really need treating. When these are properly found, the actual treatments are then often very straightforward and quick and the relief for your client will be considerable.

Always remember that your client will tell you all about the particular problems upsetting him now. You need to know about the underlying issues causing the problems and so you must always question carefully to reveal them. Don't be worried that this could take a long time in more complex cases, it is time well spent.

3. Looking for every thought field

A look at further examples: On arrival the client will say: *"I am so stressed and feel depressed."* So how are you going to proceed given this brief all encompassing information? You first thought should be: 'Why is this person stressed and depressed? It's not a normal state of living'. Indeed I know you will remind me that: 'everyone is stressed these days due to pressure of work, overload of information and intense demands on a their time stretching them to their physical and mental limits.'

Unfortunately we all know this to be the case but it doesn't make it any more acceptable just because so many are suffering from this dangerous problem. In fact it shows that we should all fully realise how this unnatural way of leading our lives has become 'normal' for so many people. And of course the great danger lies in the fact that eventually the body will complain: *"I can't cope any more so I'll make you stop"* and then physical problems arise which can sometimes be very serious, such as cancer which will finally terminate the presenting issues!

Using our gentle and effective TFT to resolve the earlier symptoms of possible major problems developing is by far the better route to a full recovery!

Thought Field Therapy

So, your asking why is this person stressed shows you are understanding that this is a totally abnormal way of living and to have any hope of returning to an acceptable existence you will have to discover the full details of the many causes of his present condition. This will inevitably be a combination of worries, anxieties, fears - even panics in certain situations and traumas. If you add this lot together it's hardly surprising that your client reports also feeling depressed!

You now have a collection of problems – which in turn result in a basketful of thought fields – that all have their perturbations sitting up waiting to be addressed! Now the really important part of your work is finding each and every thought field that needs resolution. Don't be fobbed off with: *"Oh I'm worried and anxious about everything."*

In other words your client won't appreciate the need to be specific at first; he'll simply think that the whole lot is 'the problem.'

However, we know that what the client regards as 'the problem' must be broken down into the many thought fields that, when put together, will indeed make up 'the problem.'

So, here your really vital questioning begins. Having established there are many worries and anxieties involved, begin putting the details on them. For example: *"What causes the most worry? Your boss, because she doesn't value your work even though you have been in this job for many years and know exactly what you are doing. She also puts unnecessary pressure on your time by demanding stupid reports on the progress of your department"* - etc, etc. This and its myriad variations are so common in the commercial world. With further questioning, the client in this example will come up with several more concerns over his boss at work and each one will be a unique thought field needing treatment.

Avoid the temptation to save time by lumping the whole lot under one heading 'my boss' and treating it as one problem while your client simply thinks of 'my boss.' Even this might give you a phoney result because your client could well be thinking simply of his 'nasty demanding boss' and this could give him a feeling of being more relaxed over the issue. But that still leaves all the other thought fields sitting in the basket untouched! Always remember that it's what the client is **thinking about** that gets treated. TFT is very precise in every way and that is why it's so powerful in targeting the very root cause or core issue of the problem being addressed - given that you have properly identified this root cause and are therefore treating the required thought field.

Having spent time and identified as many thought fields as you can find, you must then ask your client to review the 'basketful' and ask: *"Which problem from the one's we have found upsets you the most?"* Usually your client will not have any difficulty telling you and so go ahead and treat the particular worry/anxiety/fear involved. Always remember our Fear algorithm e-a-c 9g sq. will also address worries and anxieties since these are really lesser forms of fear.

Working with a group of fears you must also remember that due to their likely close association, your client may easily switch to another of these thought fields and you will suddenly find the SUD has increased. Immediately question what is *now* being thought about and get your

Thought Field Therapy

client back on track or go with him and start with the next thought field.

Since stress will involve at least several if not many problems, do remember that there will usually be a limit to how much treatment your client can cope with during a single session. Yes it's nice to charge ahead and remove as many upsets as you can before running out of time! - but is that fair to your client? The poor person may well be flagging after working with three or four problems and need to stop.

It's also necessary to realise this is an on-going group of problems. Typically when our client above starts work again, although he may now feel far more confident about boss, it's quite likely that boss will come up with some variation of a previous demand which will be different enough from previous ones to cause a fresh thought field complete with it's new perturbations needing attention if further upset is to be avoided.

This of course is where your sending the client away with full instructions on how to treat himself in these circumstances is so important. For many it is so empowering for them to know they can do something to help themselves. Also it is these people who take the trouble to help themselves that finish up with the most successful and truly complete treatments.

4. Questions & Case Studies from students.

'Incomplete treatment'

"I have used the anxiety algorithm with a few clients - social anxiety and anxiety with relationships. When I treated for anxiety, they both become tearful and upset half way through the treatment, the anxiety has gone almost completely but there is now just sadness. The clients haven't been clear about why they are crying or feeling so upset..."

How do I treat this? Do I carry on with the anxiety algorithm, to finish? (I guessed not in the situation as the anxiety has gone). Do I use the trauma algorithm even though they cannot explain what the trauma or the thought is? Does it matter that the client cannot identify what the thought is? Is the sadness a natural mourning that has been blocked?"

My answer:

"When a person is tearful it almost always means there are past traumas involved. I think in these cases it's important to remember two main points. The first is that many people will do their best to cope with a past trauma by repressing it. This of course does nothing to heal the problem but is the best people can do to help themselves. So keeping it out of their awareness can allow them to cope with getting on with life and so when they come to you they are naturally thinking about having help with their present problems.

Thought Field Therapy

Which brings us to the second important point: you always need to address the core issue to obtain complete success. The client is only ever thinking about the presenting problems which in this case were the social and relationship anxieties. Treating these as you did will sometimes activate the core issues which are often traumas - the very upsets from the past your client has been avoiding - maybe for many years. A good repressor will have pushed a core issue trauma so far into the background that they can have difficulty in remembering what it was. "All done and dusted" they will tell you and from the emotional angle it may well not be causing any upset now but can still be affecting the physical body and so needs to be treated.

Now the core issue is the driving force behind the presenting problems. This is where questioning the client fully about their presenting problem is so vital to finding out exactly what you really need to treat. So often a person will tell you, for example: "I always feel very anxious when I go to X or see Y or do Z etc" My reaction is always to ask why. There are many situations in life where the person normally would not feel any upset and so there has to be a reason for the upset. Faced with this sort of questioning the client then has to go into their past and will come up with a vast variety of possibilities which often are traumas from childhood - which set the pattern - and give the present problem you are addressing.

With your two clients, I'm sure they started to go into their past due to the treatment you were giving because you were dealing with core issues backwards - if you see what I mean. You worked on the presenting problem which in turn activated the core issue and this produced the unexpected upset.

So finally, could I suggest that if you can see them again, talk about any connections their present problems may have to their past and try to get them filling in with more past information until you are able to see a clear connection with the present upset. I'm sure this will be a past trauma, so get them to imagine being in the past situation now and treat with the complex trauma algorithm together with anger and guilt in case one or both are present. In this way you will have them properly tuned in to their past problems which you will remember is essential if your treatment is to work. It's always what the person is thinking about that is treated.

(a). Case Study from student: 'Depressed and angry'

" J was suffering from 'depression'. She contacted me through a friend because she was beginning to be more and more angry at the people around her.

J's mother had died one year ago from cancer. Her step father died four years ago and her natural father when she was just six years old.

She wanted to deal with her anger as she thought she was coping all right with her 'depression'. We established that her anger didn't last very long, always with people close to her and, as she put it, irrational. On asking the last time she was angry, she said that she had snapped at the dog! After she realised how crazy this was, we were able to talk a little deeper and she realised that her anger was caused from the loss of her mother. She was still living in the family home alone, taking care of the Will and sale of the house. We spoke for one hour before any treatment. She centred everything around the fact that she was lonely, scared to face the future alone and how she never mourned her mother.

Thought Field Therapy

At what I believed to be her lowest point I asked for her SUD on how depressed she was feeling now. It was a SUD 9 and I then asked her to tap the majors for the depression algorithm (30g-c 9g sq.) while thinking about her depression. She reported SUD 5 . I continued with the 9g and it reduced to SUD2, then finishing with the eye-roll to complete the treatment at SUD 0. I asked her to try and feel her depression but she couldn't. Then I asked her to think about a particular task over which she was procrastinating and she was ready to do it. We tested a further three future tasks, one of which was sill concerning her. It was signing the sale of the house which was still causing her concern. Her anxiety was at SUD 6 for this and was quickly brought down to 0 using the anxiety algorithm.

I contacted J two weeks later. She was a different person. Still in the same house with papers being signed that week and feeling 'nostalgic' and comfortable. She was tapping herself for anxiety on a regular basis and her anger had disappeared overnight.

There was lots of talking with this client - listening. I was tempted to cut in earlier and tap the individual procrastinations. Something told me to hold back. Many tears came before the realisation of her depression and not facing up to the loss of her mother. I had disbelief myself that the treatment for depression would work so easily and quickly! She did say that there were days when she was 'very down' but the tapping sequence e-a-c- 9g sq. that I showed her was working every time."

My reply:

An excellent result - well done! However, I believe that J was really suffering from trauma - trauma of her mother's death together with anger (perhaps) that her mother had 'deserted' her and left her now with all the clearing up. Something like this can lead a person to feeling 'depressed' because the traumatic event (which is the main driving force behind her present problem) has been repressed in an attempt to cope with the whole situation.

Your treatment was good inasmuch you dealt with the presenting problem rather than the core issue - the trauma of her mother's death. If you had got her to imagine being at the death now she would probably give a very high SUD as she imagined herself in the well known (to her) scenario. Then while holding that thought take her through the complex trauma with anger algorithm: eb-e-a-lf-c 9g sq. In some cases this alone will solve all present problems because the driving force has gone. In other cases you will find it's still necessary to address further thought fields individually as you have done.

Your report of her having days feeling 'very down' also suggest the effect of the untreated trauma being still very much present and if you can see her again do treat this for her.

(b). Case Study from student: 'Locked in falling lift'

"Client A has an extreme fear of lifts. This occurred after being locked in a falling lift! She has been able to deal with it to a certain extent in that she is able to get into big, sturdy new lifts with at least one person.

I decided to first use the trauma algorithm to get rid of the trauma of being locked up in a falling lift and then use the fear algorithm to combat the fear. The trauma initial SUD was 5. After applying the majors, the client reported SUD 4. As this was a one point drop I decided to correct

Thought Field Therapy

for specific PR and repeat the majors. The SUD was now 3 so I continued with the 9 gamut sequence, the SUD came down to 1 and then I finished with the eye-roll. The client now looked confused but accepted what happened.

For the phobia treatment the initial SUD for the fear of lifts was 10. After the majors for the simple phobia algorithm there was no drop in SUD and so I corrected for specific PR and repeated the majors. The SUD remained unchanged at 10 so I corrected for recurring PR, repeated the majors and this time there was a two-point drop to SUD 8. Continuing with the 9 gamut sequence unfortunately did not result in a further drop in SUD. I continued with a correction for mini PR but I'm not sure if I should use this since the SUD has not dropped below the 5 point mark and most of the problem still remains. After repeating the majors now there is still no drop in SUD. I now continue with correction for PR2 and repeat the majors. To my surprise and relief the SUD drops to a 6. I continue with the 9 gamut sequence and again hit a wall - the SUD remains at 6! At this stage I decide to do collarbone breathing as my last resort. I then repeat the majors once again and the SUD drops to 4. After the 9 gamut sequence the SUD is 2. At this stage I decide the treatment has been completed and do the eye-roll which brings the SUD to 1.

Even though the trauma treatment worked, the client was adamant that the fear will not go away. When the SUD was not dropping I could see the 'I told you so' look. The client patiently put up with me. Once the SUD dropped after the collarbone breathing, the look of confusion was evident. When we finished she was trying very hard to feel the fear and all that she said was that the feeling was very weird! This treatment took place some months ago and since then she has been able to get into lifts she could not enter before. I spoke to her recently and it seems she is unable to get into the small lifts again. I assume the presence of a toxin has partially reversed the treatment.

My reply:

Certainly you were absolutely right first to address the root cause of her fears - the trauma of being 'locked in a falling lift. ' It sounds quite horrific! Your treatment was excellent and I presume you used the complex trauma algorithm? However since it must have been such an upsetting incident, I'm a little surprised that her initial SUD was only 5? Either it happened many years ago (you don't mention how long) and she has been able successfully to repress the problem, or there are still further aspects of the incident which have not been addressed. Multiple traumas in cases like this are quite usual and you need to find them by discussing fully with the client exactly what happened and so discover all the thought fields that need to be resolved. Otherwise you still have several 'onion layers' remaining.

Moving into the present time with her phobic fear next is fine - but you did struggle! ! I think there are two most likely reasons. The first is your choice of algorithm. You have not told me precisely the algorithm you used, but you indicated that it was the normal 'fear algorithm to combat the fear'. By this I presume you mean: e-a-c 9g sq.?

BUT you are dealing with claustrophobia! This together with spiders and turbulence must be treated with the alternative sequence: a-e-c 9g sq.

Thought Field Therapy

If on the other hand you were using the correct algorithm, then the most likely reason is due to an initial incomplete treatment of the trauma as I've shown. Although she would have been thinking of being in a lift during your phobia treatment, it is most likely her mind would have strayed on to a past traumatic aspect not treated previously and hence you are struggling with the wrong algorithm. This also tends to be confirmed by the fact that even now she still has trouble with small lifts - the size of the original faulty one?

Your protocol throughout was very good. You didn't get lost, and worked through all the PR corrections in turn very well indeed and eventually got there! Well done!

(c). Case Study from student: 'The underlying stammer'

For 18 months I have been coaching this young man using my coaching and NLP skills. During that time he has progressed fantastically from being totally insecure, living at home with mum, never having a girlfriend or any sexual relationships, in a part time job earning £11k pa. - with no real plans or hopes for the future and basically hating himself - to a confident person sharing a flat with two girls, in a new fulfilling job earning £18k pa. and really liking himself!

Two weeks ago he surprised me by admitting that he had suffered with a stammer for most of his life. He had developed some amazing strategies to disguise it as I was completely unaware. Basically he substituted words or completely avoided using them. I did some initial work with him and developed some simplified coping strategies. This week at my session he had progressed very well and was able to say all the difficult words without much of a problem - until I 'put the pressure on' by getting him to imagine being in front of his workmates reading out the list. He said he was feeling anxious and of course stammered even with the strategy in place. He said he felt hot, sweaty and sick and wanted to run away!

I then talked to him about TFT and introduced the idea that we could use it to deal with his problem. He agreed to give it a try. I decided to use the panic/anxiety algorithm: eb-e-a-c 9g sq. I planned this as he had told me he felt anxious and was almost panicky when he thought of speaking in front of his workmates, who he thought would think he was a 'spastic' if he stammered with his words.

Having talked to him about his great anxiety he gave an initial SUD of 9. I did the majors and got a good reduction to SUD 6. Then I did the 9g and his score did not move. (I then realised I had omitted the gamut point tapping!) so I did a *repeat 9g correctly* and his score moved to a 5. As it had moved only one point I did a specific PR which moved the SUD to a 4. then I repeated the majors and it moved to a 3, then I repeated the 9g but it remained at a 3 so I tried a Mini PR and it still remained at 3 so I then did PR2 which moved it to a 2. Relieved! I then applied Collarbone Breathing and the score moved to a 1. Then I finished the sequence with an eye-roll which he seemed to enjoy!

Apex statement: "I don't really think it was a 9 to start with." Classic really! !

Client comments: "Tapping really works. I don't need to be anxious any more. I can say all the words - I don't need to worry. Two weeks ago you said we could fix this and

Thought Field Therapy

I did not believe it was possible. To have come so far in that time is fantastic! "

Student comments: I am completely thrilled with this as I was not sure how I could really help him but the TFT very quickly removed the last blockage (or should I say lump!) I am really seeing the power of combining my NLP coaching and TFT skills together.

My reply:

Very good work with a lovely result. Thank you for the classic Apex - nicely proving how necessary it is to write down the initial SUD! A major part of your successes as shown in all three of your studies, is your ability to find just the right thought field which needs to be addressed. You may remember I said that this is probably up to 75% of the final success rate achieved and can push your algorithm results beyond the stated 80%.

In this case, having discovered his stammer, you got him nicely into a situation of great fear and realised it was then panic. So the algorithm was fine but the protocol went a bit haywire causing you to struggle a little. Starting with SUD 9 and arriving at 6 after the majors is good and you correctly carried on with the 9g. Forgetting your little peccadillo where you forgot the gamut spot! - you arrived at SUD 5 and properly corrected with side of hand PR correction.

Now at this point you do not ask again for the SUD because there is no good reason why it should have changed. Remember that doing a PR correction makes it now possible for the next part of your treatment to work. Therefore you immediately repeat the majors and **then** ask for the SUD at which point you can reasonably expect the possibility that it has now gone down. If not, you should then proceed to the next PR correction - Recurring PR - and again repeat the majors before asking once more for the SUD. In the event, when you did repeat the majors, your PR correction actually reduced the SUD from 6 to 3!

After this you got back on track with the Mini PR but I don't really understand why this did not reduce the SUD again. Are you sure the client was properly thinking only of the little bit of problem remaining, or was his mind tending to wander off into an associated thought field?

Whatever happened it seems the PR2 correction did the trick and you were nicely at SUD 2. Please do not now launch into a full blown CB2 treatment! ! Once a SUD is down to 2 - always do the eye roll. The eye roll will hardly ever fail to bring a 2 down to 1. And you can test this for yourself - ask the client after reporting a SUD 1- 'are you sure that all upset has gone or is there something which is still able to bother you a little? ' The answer is invariably - 'no it really has all gone' The eye roll is a great little chap - don't underestimate its great ability to complete a treatment vey quickly and efficiently. And remember to use it to consolidate and finish a treatment already at a SUD 1. Oh and do tell people to use it totally on its own as a great rapid relaxation technique! They will enjoy it!

4. Anxiety and Fear

1. What is Anxiety?
2. What is Fear?
3. Understanding Anxiety & Fear
4. Treating Anxiety and Fear

1. What is Anxiety?

Anxiety is surprisingly difficult to pin down in terms of an absolute definition but in generalised terms it is described as a rather vague but clearly disagreeable emotional state that may also be associated with varying degrees of apprehension, dread, stress and agitation. Physically, the sufferer may also experience "malaise" - once again an undefined sensation of "just not feeling well".

Worry and uneasiness predominate although there is often no identifiable precipitating factor. The sufferer always seems to be anticipating the worst, expressing exaggerated concerns about health, money, family, or work. Additionally, those concerns are largely seen to be uncontrollable or unavoidable.

Typical signs and symptoms include:

- Restlessness and / or edginess
- Rumination of problems

- Inability to concentrate for periods of time.
- Irritability.
- Muscular tension.
- Fatigue but problems with sleeping (initial insomnia or restlessness, rumination of thoughts preventing sleep, etc.).

These can lead to clinically important impairments of home, personal and social interactions as well as those of employment.

If there is no identifiable cause, and three or more of the above are present for at least half the days in a given six month period, then the subject may be suffering from Generalised Anxiety Disorder.

2. What is Fear?

Unlike anxiety, fear is a normal emotional state caused by a perceived threat to one's well being and almost always relates to what the consequence of that threat will be. Essentially, fear prepares us for escape, avoidance or handling of a continuing or worsening fearful situation - the "fight or flight" reaction.

As such, fear should be clearly distinguished from anxiety which occurs without external threat and with helplessness as a feature.

Fear only becomes a problem if this normal response is triggered by something that a reasonable observer would regard as harmless and therefore poses no threat to well being. When this occurs the subject is said to have a phobia. Phobias are discussed in Chapter 9.

3. Understanding Anxiety & Fear

Have you ever felt anxious or fearful? What a daft question! None of us can go through life without experiencing these very common emotions. It is because these emotions are so prevalent throughout life that the question is obviously ridiculous.

But why are anxiety and fear such a normal part of our lives? It is because in it's most basic form it is nature's way of protecting us. As such we all exhibit exactly the same reaction to given situations both mentally and physically. Lets look at the well known Fight or Flight syndrome. If you and I go out together into the garden and suddenly spot a large tiger just behind a bush, we will instantly both have identical mind and body reactions: Immediately enormous fear will take over our thoughts to the exclusion of everything else so that we can furiously work out what to do - fast!

Also we will both exhibit identical body reactions: The pupils in the eyes will constrict, skin vessels constrict so that it goes white since blood supply is increased to muscles, brain and heart. There is increased blood supply to vital organs and there is a release of adrenaline. **The body is following a set of instructions.**

Dr. Callahan explains that it is this very specific reaction to fear - or anger, or guilt etc. that is shared by all members of the species and is a highly ordered reaction. If it happened from disorder or disturbance, it would not be possible to obtain order from it. Also any medical problem shows a standard set of symptoms for a particular illness. This again is the body following instructions to cope with the invader and eliminate it from the system.

This realisation that fear is the major 'tool' of nature to protect us - and animals - is shown in the natural phobic fear of babies who crawl and will carefully avoid any perceived deep drop nearby. Also this protective phobic fear for the young is shown by Hornbills who are North American birds that build their nests in hollow trees. As the young hornbills mature, they have to chip open the protective covering to their nest to be able to be able to get out to fledge.

In an amazing film there were three hornbill youngsters laid and hatched just 48 hours apart. The behaviour of the chicks was radically different due to the slight differences in their age.

The oldest overcame his fear of opening the closure and in order to get out begins chipping away at the hole. The second oldest boldly attempted to stop the older chick from opening the hole and tried to close it up again (droppings are used for this purpose). But it's easier to open than close, and the older chick wins out and escapes to fledge.

The next older chick, No2 then patches up the hole.

While this drama is going on, the youngest chick No3 is shivering with obvious fear in the far corner of the hollow!

Just 48 hours difference in age causes the radical difference in the three distinct behaviours: Aggressive No1 opens the hole. Aggressive, in another way No2 attempts to close it; while the youngest baby chick No3 huddles with fear in the far corner of the nest getting as far away as possible from the upsetting activity.

Thought Field Therapy

SO - in TFT terms, we believe that the perturbations in the perceptual field causing fear was active until a certain age. At the critical age, this perturbation is subsumed naturally (you might call it a **natural psychotherapy**) and the chicks can go ahead with little or no fear.

This is a very clear example of maturity or age having a direct effect on fear (or perturbations). Two days or 48 hours separate each chick. The two oldest do not experience fear at the opening when they reach the appropriate age of maturity, but the youngest does. Four days after the first chick left and two days after the second chick left, the lone-baby has no fear and opens up the hole itself so it can get out and fledge.

The young of all animals automatically experience fear in certain situations and the purpose of this natural fear is to protect them from common dangers.

From these two examples of Phobic Fear and the Direct Fear (in the presence of a tiger) we see the **constructive** use of this very powerful emotion and treatment is not normally needed - except in the case of a phobic fear that is not naturally subsumed with maturation - and so we have to do the job that nature has failed to do for some individuals. This fear is also constructive in that the body and mind expend the instant pent up energy by quickly taking action which totally resolves the situation and all systems return to normal.

Now let me ask you a question which is not quite so daft! Do you tend to worry a lot? Are you anxious about certain things at the moment? Are you fearful that particular happenings will take place in the near or not-so-near future that could have a major impact on your life? Are you under great pressure and feeling totally stressed! ?

I would be very surprised if you did not answer yes to at least one of these possibilities.

So here again we see the prevalent use of fear in our daily lives BUT this is mainly **destructive** fear. A very different 'animal' to the constructive version. And it is so destructive because it is an **unresolved** fear. It is a fear that builds in the body and mind since there is no release for it. As such it becomes well established and so increases the internal tension to produce a chronic condition which is often called stress. We all know that stress can literally be a killer because if no action is taken to change the situation and release the pent up preparedness of the body to address the fears involved, then the physical body will simple have to force the needed action by becoming ill. In severe cases this can easily mean cancer and heart problems.

However before things become so acute, the body will send out warning signals such as extreme tiredness and a lack of energy. Also sometimes a lack of appetite and an awareness that there is continual worrying about this, that and everything else! This is where it's essential to listen to your body, take note and **do** something about your present situation. So often people will think: 'Oh! I don't feel very well, but I can cope because I have to cope' Without putting too fine a point on it - this could be signing your own death warrant!

Even here we can see how nature is using fear to do its best to protect us! BUT we have to be listening and not automatically rejecting any attempt to change our situation and so resolve the problem. Unlike the 'tiger' the possibility of a wrong resolution is not imminent and

Thought Field Therapy

therefore can be deferred indefinitely. But in this case the delay itself can be catastrophic!

4. Treating Anxiety & Fear

Now you can understand that treating fear can be a complex undertaking! Yes - there are the simple straightforward fears such as spiders, deep water or anxiety over the job interview next week. These simple (to TFT practitioners) cases were the favourites of a GP who once trained with me and remembering the small amount of time he can afford each patient, told me: "I like TFT because it nicely fits my 10 minute rule." He was so aware that he could actually send a patient away completely cured in just 10 minutes (or less! !) Then he added: "It's better than reaching for the prescription pad! " I assured him: "You've got the right idea! "

I wish there were many more GPs like this one!

In most cases your anxious or fearful client will present with a 'basket full' of problems that we must remember all have their own thought fields with their own perturbations sitting up 'bright and bushy-tailed' waiting to wreak their havoc once attuned - thought about. I have said anxious or fearful since the algorithm for treating both is the same - as it is for phobic fear. Anxiety is usually a milder and less focused reaction which as it becomes more intense will progress into full blown fear. If you're not sure which you are dealing with for a particular client, don't worry. Simply go ahead with your anxiety/fear algorithm for a positive result.

BUT - this is where your investigation into your client's 'basket' is so important before you attempt to treat anything. Remember that the client will usually come with his own idea of what needs to be treated and you will find the person is very good at telling you all about their presenting problems. Don't follow these ideas! The thought that should be uppermost in your mind should be: 'Why does this person have these problems? In most cases they are not natural and so must be present now for a reason'. Therefore you spend time (forget any 10 minute rules now!) to talk to your client and ask questions to lead their thought back to the possible causes of their present troubles. Sometimes this will 'open the floodgates' and you will receive a torrent of information about - everything! Although we know the client has a 'basket full of separate problems, the client will usually think of them globally as just 'my problem' treating it as a single entity.

So during what may become a lengthy torrent of information, listen carefully for the relevant parts that indicate the presence of a thought field and tick them off in your mind as they fly by you. If you can find time to make some quick notes, so much the better. As previously mentioned, I once treated a woman with a multiple anxiety disorder who, once I got her going, simply would not stop! ! I tried many times to get into her conversation but failed! After half an hour of non-stop listening to mainly irrelevant chat, I had to say - as kindly as I could: "Please will you stop talking as otherwise I will not be able to help you! " She stopped and actually listened for a change and we made some meaningful progress!

In most cases of course, you will be able to discuss the various fears and anxieties with your client and more often than not you will find some of the present fears started a long time ago - even in childhood - a traumatic

Thought Field Therapy

incident or related traumatic incidents. So here you will have found the core issue which is the driving force behind the present fear/s etc. If you treat only the present fear for the client, then he will certainly feel better, but since the core issue trauma/s is still in place, the current fear is likely to resurface, albeit in a slightly different form - thus representing a fresh, but closely related thought field. So always look for the core issues driving the person's problem and taking the person back in his mind to the actual trauma/s, get a SUD (which will often be present to the client's surprise) and treat with your complex trauma algorithm or if necessary with our favourite 'catch all' complex trauma with anger and guilt. As with all traumas, keep a look out for switching to associated traumas that are part of the overall trouble.

Students often ask me: *"Where do you start when presented with a full basket?"* Resisting the temptation to reply: *"At the beginning, go on to the end and then stop"*!! I always suggest the best plan is to ask the client. So assuming you have discovered and cleared any core-issue traumas first, say to your client: "Thinking of the fears and anxieties we have been talking about, which one would you say upsets you the most? " Usually a person has no difficulty in indentifying this and you will probably find it is the one you would have chosen yourself. If on the other hand the answer is a surprise to you since you believed this one was a more minor problem, ask the client why, in particular is this anxiety so very upsetting to you? This will probably elicit further explanation showing why this problem is obviously the most upsetting by giving you previously withheld information.

So you go ahead treating the selected thought field with the well known algorithm, **e - a - c 9g sq** reminding the client to be sure to think **only** of the particular anxiety now being addressed to the exclusion of all the others. This is most important because as you know, TFT can only deal with one thought field at a time and these clients, being so used to thinking of the whole 'basketful' as their one problem, can sometimes have great difficulty in thinking of only the one aspect. So if the start of your treatment is rapidly getting nowhere, stop and ask your client: *"Are you still thinking only of xyz that we were talking about a few minutes ago? "* Very often you will have the answer: *"Yes I am, but I'm also thinking about abc! "* Translated this means I'm not thinking about xyz any more but concentrating on many of my problems (as is the person's habit)! So now you will need to spend some time explaining to your client why it is so important that he thinks only about the particular anxiety or fear identified if your are going to be able to resolve it. Now start again having your person really concentrating on the precise problem and again giving you a starting SUD. If he is successful you will make progress with the algorithm this time - but still beware! - because the person is extremely likely to switch to another thought field as you reduce the SUD on the original one. So be ready to spot this and go with it. Continue this way as far as possible - meaning either the client runs out of thought fields to treat; you run out of time for this appointment; or the client is too weary and showing signs of tiredness and needing to stop. The first reason to stop treatment is excellent because you now have a happy client aware that his problems are over - at least for the time being. Obviously time has to be a consideration, especially if you're running a busy clinic. See the person again very soon if at all possible and never leave anyone half way through an algorithm. Whatever it takes, be sure to complete the particular thought field being addressed before the person leaves.

Finally the client being too tired to carry on. Never push a person who has 'reached the end of the road' as far as full attention is concerned. Remember that a TFT treatment will shift a great deal of energy - fast. This is because we are using the body's energy through working on the meridians to address the perturbations in the thought field. In some cases, particularly where you are working with a deep emotion the client is often left feeling very weary and so is grateful to stop treatment for now. Don't forget that this invariably shows your treatment has been very successful and this will be clearly confirmed by the person's facial expression and body language.

Continue your good work on any further visits. The whole process is well described as the 'onion skin principle'. The outer layer is the most upsetting thought field that you dealt with first. Then you move down one to the second layer and remove that. Continuing this way you will eventually remove the last layer and at that point your client knows that his problem has gone. Before the last layer is removed, we can say this person 'still has an onion'!

Now it's important to be aware that the outer layers, while they are still in place, will suppress the lower layers sometimes to such an extent that the person will not be aware of them even after the outer layers have gone. Then the client does become aware of their effect a few days later as they move into the uppermost position. If you haven't made a firm second booking with this person, then he will now conclude that: 'Well TFT was good while it lasted - but of course it doesn't really work for me'!

Your person has not realised that it's a new thought field, closely associated with the previous ones, that being so far untreated are now causing the upset.

A good way of explaining this phenomenon to clients having multiple problems is given to us by Dr. Roger Callahan in his nice little story called:

Tooth - Shoe - Lump

A person has a terrible toothache. He calls the dentist and rushes over to the surgery.

Although there is no opening for an appointment, the dentist promises to take care of the problem as soon as she can.

The tooth was hurting so much, the patient put on the first available pair of shoes, ignoring the fact that these shoes hurt his feet. Due to the intense tooth pain however, he doesn't notice the discomfort caused by the shoes.

When he gets to the surgery he sits on a couch directly on a most uncomfortable lump! Again, this goes unnoticed because of the severe tooth pain.

Just then the dentist comes out to indicate she will be able to attend to the problem in about an hour and a half. However the seeing the awful severity of the pain, she quickly injects a shot of Novocain to give temporary relief.

The tooth being suddenly relieved of all pain, the patient now becomes aware he put on the wrong shoes and realises his feet are quite uncomfortable. He removes the offending shoes and in a moment begins to be aware of the uncomfortable lump on which he has been sitting. He moves to a nearby chair and, at last, feels comfortable!

Thought Field Therapy

Something similar to this occurs in some severely complex cases who are only aware of the summation effect of their problems and are not able to discriminate between say, trauma, anxiety and depression, or a mixture of various other problems.

By contrast, other people who only have a string of more simple anxieties without any particular core issues being involved, are quite happy to plough on from thought field to thought field without any difficulty. I once treated a man who assured me he did suffer from many anxieties in his life, but he did not want to tell me anything about them. So again because we are using the wonders of TFT, my treatment was not held up at all. I asked him to think of the anxiety that upset him the most - outer onion layer - and said: "I'm going to call this Anxiety No 1." So while he was busy thinking about No1. I ran him through the anxiety algorithm asking for the SUDS as normal. He came down to a SUD 1 without any difficulty which clearly showed in his manner. We then moved on to Anxiety No2 and repeated the process with a similar satisfactory result. Reminding him that he must remember what Nos. 1 and 2 and 3 etc. actually meant we finally completed seven different thought fields and he was happy that all his problems had gone. He was 'chirpy as a cricket ' after we'd finished and showed no sign of tiredness!

Nevertheless about three months later, he rang me to explain that he was again suffering from anxiety and wanted to see me because he was confident I could resolve his problem again. Great to have someone who really understood that TFT is a brilliant therapy and not 'just a quick fix'! ! He came with further 'secret' anxieties all neatly numbered and we worked through them as before without any problems.

He left feeling very happy with the result and I never heard from him again! To this day I have absolutely no idea what his anxieties were about!

So let us again remind ourselves of one of the unique wonders of TFT lest we should grow to take it for granted! You, as the TFT practitioner, do not have to know anything about your client's problem providing (at the algorithm level) you know enough to put it in the correct category for treatment.

For many people this is an enormous boon since having to talk about their problem will often put the person off looking for any treatment in the first place. Also as we've seen with trauma, talking about the upsetting experience is the worst possible treatment. Always remember: It's what the **person is thinking about** during treatment that gets treated. Exactly what you are thinking about is not relevant although you obviously need to be concentrating on the treatment you're giving. In theory you could be thinking about lying in the sun on a tropical beach beside a blue lagoon! ! - but as a serious practitioner this would be disastrous.!

Unlike past traumatic experiences which are not usually affected by the presence of toxins, you will find that the treatment of multiple anxieties and fears are quite often held up by substances specifically toxic to the client. This is not a problem if you have been trained in how to diagnose and treat toxins and so negate their effect.

We must always remember that multiple anxiety can develop into a habit. So if you find your person has a habit of worrying about everything and anything, then you must realise that he has an OCD to worry. This person will have an obsessive need to worry - literally about

Thought Field Therapy

anything. So you must give your client the full addiction treatment to target his need to be anxious. Start as always by addressing the need to indulge now - the need to 'do a worry' and get a SUD for it. As with the treatment for addiction to a substance, you will find this treatment of the desire/need to indulge in being anxious is very effective. In the more extreme cases, after this treatment your client will suddenly realise he is not actually worrying at the moment, and will then promptly start to worry that he is not worrying about anything! So treat that one as well!

As with all addictions, it is imperative the client follows your full instructions for addressing the OCD by continuing the treatment at home and expect the complete resolution to take three weeks or more. Be sure to organise a repeat visit within the next 7 days to check on progress and also look again for possible undisclosed core issues that will need your further treatment.

5. Panic Attacks and Panic Disorder

1. What are Panic Attacks?
2. What is Panic Disorder?
3. Understanding Panic Disorder
4. Treating Panic Disorder

1. What are Panic Attacks?

Panic is defined as a sudden overwhelming fear, with or without cause, that produces hysterical or irrational behaviour, and that often spreads quickly through a group of persons in the same situation.

However, panic attacks are individually experienced as feelings of extreme apprehension, often terror, with sudden and unexplainable onset. Sufferers get no warning of an attack and are unable to predict when an attack will occur. As a consequence, those affected may also develop signs and symptoms of generalised anxiety or acute traumatic stress as the experience can be very traumatic. The most common description given by those who experience panic attacks is that they feel as if they are about to die.

Thought Field Therapy

In addition, specific or generalised phobias may also arise, with the focus on places or situations where panic attacks have occurred. For example, if a sufferer always has panic attacks away from home they may develop agoraphobia; they become intensely fearful about being in a place or situation from which escape would be difficult or embarrassing, or if a panic attack occurred, rapid support might not be available. Similarly, if panic attacks become associated with enclosed spaces, such as in a passenger lift, the sufferer may develop claustrophobia.

Typical signs and symptoms of panic include:

- Chest pain and / or tightening,
- Cold sweats or hot flushes,
- A choking or smothering sensation with perceived shortness of breath,
- Feelings of unreality or of being detached from oneself,
- Light-headedness, feeling faint or dizzy,
- Fear of dying,
- Fear of loss of control or becoming insane,
- Rapid pounding heart beat which may be felt or seen in the chest,
- Perceived skipped heart beats,
- Nausea,
- Numbness or tingling in the extremities and / or cheeks,
- Pronounced trembling,

- Inability to focus thoughts or think rationally,
- Inability to make immediate decisions.

It should be noted that in the vast majority of cases panic attacks do subside spontaneously with no lasting physiological or emotional consequences. It is almost inevitable that everyone will experience a panic attack at least once in their lifetime, no remedial treatment ever being necessary.

However, the residual feelings of distress and exhaustion that come with repeated attacks can be enough to affect the sufferer's personal, social and work life.

2. What is Panic Disorder?

If the subject has recurrent and unexpected panic attacks, and for a month or more after at least one of these attacks has experienced one or more of:

- Ongoing concern that they will have more attacks.
- Worry as to the cause of the attacks or their impact on well-being or life-expectancy
- Significant change in everyday behaviour, such as avoidance of situations or places.

then the subject may be suffering from Panic Disorder.

3. Understanding Panic Disorder

Panic is an extreme version of fear. Being an extreme condition it will often develop from a fearful situation becoming worse or very often suddenly take over the person's senses both mental and physical so as to render him temporarily unable to function properly. This condition is usually caused by past traumatic memories being suddenly triggered by any stimulus such as seeing or hearing something which was previously present at the original happening. Even a smell such as perfume on the perfumery counter or the stench of the supermarket detergent aisle could trigger an attack because the smell was produced by a product toxic to the person.

As always a person will use coping techniques to avoid having panic attacks, by not thinking about the triggering situations, (keep them under the carpet!) or knowing what will trigger the problem, will keep away from those situations: "I daren't drive down the slipway because as soon as I'm on the motorway, I know I will panic and then struggle to get across on to the hard shoulder where I can stop and try to compose myself before starting off again." Obviously these poor people can be a danger to themselves and others if caught having a panic attack in this situation.

And then of course there's the Corporal Jones' of Dad's Army way of 'coping' when he's suddenly in great fear: "Don't Panic - Don't Panic! ! "

4. Treating Panic Disorder

Complex Anxiety and Panic are treated together because the one will be present with the other. Yes, the person may simply be anxious or fearful at first and so can keep control of the situation. But then due to a trigger or the intensity of the problem increasing, then the panic can quickly set in and take over. So here you need to be sure of what you are working with. Ask your client: "When xyz happens, are you anxious or do you become really fearful? " "Yes, I'm usually very anxious because ….." So you treat the anxiety. If it really was fear the person suffered it would not matter because the same algorithm treats both. So you win either way!

But if the answer was: "Well, I do get really fearful" then you need to ask further:

"When you feel so fearful, does that sometimes become a panic? " If the answer now is yes, then you must use a panic algorithm - which is different to the fear algorithm. There are six algorithms for panic and I find the first one:

eb -e -a -c 9g sq. is usually very effective. Now you will notice that this is not only the algorithm for Complex Trauma, but that it is identical to the fear algorithm **except** for the critical initial eb (eyebrow) point. So if you have the situation where your client is not really sure if his fear develops into panic at any time, then use the panic algorithm. If his problem is just straight fear, then TFT will simply ignore the unnecessary eyebrow point and your treatment will be successful.

Thought Field Therapy

Always expect the 'full basket' of fears where panics are present. Also remember to ask the questions - why and when? "When did you first begin to panic over xyz and why does it still affect you now? " You are looking for the core issue again and finding the past traumatic experience causing the present problems. There may be several of these in the 'larger baskets' so be sure to question all clients and take them back into their pasts so that you can make a thorough search for possible causes of all problems. As ever, treat these first to remove their effects before treating the present issues.

Also as with multiple anxieties and fears, there is always the chance of Individual Energy Toxins being present and 'holding up the works.' If this happens you will need to diagnose and treat any toxins blocking your healing progress.

Agoraphobics can be quite tricky to help - not least because they are not capable of coming to see you. The journey is much too scary. So, if you can, go to their house and expect to see them several times. This is because you will usually find complex anxiety over many issues - each of which will have it's own perturbation.

Also you will find panic and probably trauma.

Thinking of all the agoraphobic's problems as 'trees in a forest' there is the temptation to charge in and cut the trees down one by one until you have cleared the ground. BUT you will find this approach much too frightening for this phobic, and so it is better to try gently lopping off the tops of all the trees so that the person can begin to see around a little better and then later having another session to lower them further, and so on. You will find this approach much more acceptable. In terms of SUD levels, be content initially with lowering SUDS from (say) 10 to 8 for every thought field treated and later hopefully to 6 or 5 and so on.

Remembering that these people have shut themselves away in a self- imposed prison for - maybe years, you cannot expect them suddenly to bust out into the outside world after the odd TFT treatment or two! You will need to address their multiple traumas and associated panics straight away as far as possible on each visit and above all, be sure to show your client how to treat himself in between your visits. The really successful outcomes for these phobics is amongst those who really work at self treatment. By working with you this way the 'trees' are gradually lowered more quickly and your client is aware that things are becoming less scary so that actually taking a short walk or going to the supermarket with the help of a friend becomes a real possibility. It is then the person knows a final cure to their debilitating problem is now in sight.

In all cases giving clients full information in how to treat themselves is very empowering for many. They now know they can do something very effective to help themselves overcome their problems which they find much preferable to having yet another pill to take because the doctor says it will help! TFT cannot leave any side-effects!

6. Trauma and PTSD

1. What is Acute Stress Disorder?
2. What is Post Traumatic Stress Disorder?
3. TFT and Traumatic Stress
4. Treating Traumatic Stress
5. Case Studies

1. What is Acute Stress Disorder?

Acute Stress Disorder (ASD) is a relatively moderate incapacitating condition that follows an event that terrifies a person. Typically, that person experienced, witnessed or was confronted with circumstances that led to death or serious injury, or led them to believe that death or serious injury to themselves or others was imminent. The person will also report that they experienced feelings of extreme fear, helplessness or horror.

In ASD, onset of symptoms is immediate or arises within four weeks. Those symptoms will last for a minimum of two days but very rarely last more than four weeks and progressive recovery is the norm.

Immediate symptoms include a sense of numbing or detachment from the situation ("this can't be happening") typified by an apparent absence of emotional responsiveness. The individual may also comment that they felt "in a daze" and find it difficult to recall significant aspects of the traumatising event, both of which indicate a degree of dissociation or depersonalisation.

During this period, the person may also experience recurrent thoughts, dreams or flashbacks, exhibit distress on being reminded of the event (in conversation, for example), or may even have a disturbing sense of reliving the entire experience. As a consequence, avoidance behaviour will be evident, the individual deliberately keeping themselves away from thoughts, conversations, activities, people and places associated with the event.

A sufferer of ASD will typically:

relive the event in at least one of these ways:

- Intrusive, distressing recollections - thoughts, images.
- Repeated, distressing dreams.
- Through flashbacks, hallucinations or illusions, acts or feels as if the event were recurring.
- Marked mental distress in reaction to internal or external cues that symbolise or resemble the event.
- Physiological reactivity - such as rapid heart beat, elevated blood pressure in response to these cues.

demonstrate avoidance behaviour involving at least three of the following:

- tries to avoid thoughts, feelings or conversations concerned with the event;

Thought Field Therapy

- tries to avoid activities, people or places that recall the event;
- cannot recall an important feature of the event;
- marked loss of interest or participation in activities important to the person;
- feels detached or isolated from other people;
- feels restricted in their ability to love or feel other strong emotions;
- feels that life will now be brief and/or unfulfilled.

Have his or her everyday life affected to such an extent that it causes undue distress or impairs work, social or personal functioning in at least two of these ways:

- Insomnia (initial or interval)
- Irritability
- Poor concentration
- Hypervigilance
- Increased startle response

2. What is Post Traumatic Stress Disorder?

As with ASD, a person will have experienced, witnessed or have been confronted with circumstances that led to death or serious injury, or will have led them to believe that death or serious injury to themselves or others was imminent.

However, the typical symptomology described above will have progressed beyond four weeks and have shown little or no diminution in severity.[6] Those symptoms may also not have arisen for an extended period of time following the trauma (be it several weeks, months or even years), but be triggered by another event.

3. TFT and Traumatic Stress

Trauma plays a very important part in the theoretical understanding of psychological problems and their treatment.

Trauma is a unique class of problem because it consists of a perfectly normal, appropriate emotional reaction to an objectively terrible situation or event. In the majority of cases, the victim experiences a period of intense distress lasting anything from a few hours or days, followed by a period of up to a month with progressively diminishing symptoms. No intervention, other than perhaps the ministrations of friends and family, is necessary.

However, it is most interesting that it is possible with TFT to banish all emotional upset over a very real objective trauma almost immediately.

---

[6] The therapist should note that the distinction between ASD and PTSD depends on time not severity

Thought Field Therapy

Dr. Callahan believes that the importance of this intriguing fact suggests something most surprising about Nature - that Nature's programme gives us licence, an invitation to be relatively free of intense emotional upset over very real horrible events.

The ease and simplicity of TFT are startling and provide strong support for our theoretical notions of the perturbation. Knowing what to do (i.e. using the specific TFT algorithms which address the fundamental causal aspects of emotional disturbance) makes it rather easy to eliminate most symptoms of traumatic stress.

TFT offers a very pro-quality of life gift. The choice of increased personal freedom is remarkable.

Some of the most common causes of traumatic stress you are likely to experience with your clients are: Love-pain, Rejection, Bereavement, Crime, War, Accident, Natural Disaster, and Surgical Procedures.

Many people believe that once they have experienced a traumatic event, then they will have to learn to cope and live with it for the rest of their lives. Unfortunately without the intervention of TFT this is often true! There are still psychologists who believe this and others who say the only way to address this problem is to find some way to remove the memory of the traumatic event!

This obviously cannot be done since it's not possible to lose the memory of an actual major event which took place in one's life, unless traumatic amnesia has occurred. Nor is it acceptable to consider losing the memory of a precious child or cherished partner who has died!

Another very unfortunate, yet clinically accepted, way to cope with trauma is to give the person counselling as soon as possible after the event. This is often a counter-productive approach because the last thing a traumatised person really wants to do is talk about their terrible experience!

Left alone over a period of time, most people are able to find a coping technique which enables them to resolve their distress naturally. Sometimes, this is not successful and other strategies are adopted (avoidance, for example) which tend to 'keep the problem under the carpet'. They still harbour some distress but manage to lead as normal a life as possible. This residual distress surfaces occasionally, help is sought, and along comes the well-meaning counselling therapist pulling all the terrible memories from their place under the carpet and stirring up fresh distress!

Not helpful! It was in January 2000 that the warning was given at the British Psychological Association conference in Brighton, following research commissioned by the Health and Safety Executive. After analysing the results of seven random controlled trials, the researchers - from Birkbeck College, London, and the University of Sussex - found there was no evidence that debriefing helped victims in the long term but there was evidence that it had harmed them. "At best its efficacy is neutral and at worst it can be damaging," said Jo Ricks, principal research fellow at the institute of employment studies at the University of Sussex.

4. Treating Traumatic Stress

So how do we tackle this problem with TFT? First and foremost the **client does not have to talk in detail about**

their traumatic experience! As we know it is necessary only for the person to be **thinking** about the problem to be able to treat it with TFT. This will tune the thought field and the perturbations in that thought field will be active **at that time**. Remember we are addressing only the perturbations in the thought field and removing them from activity. This means that the memory of the trauma is not touched - only the emotional upset has gone. All is the same except for the upset.

After treatment, most people find that their recall of the past event is even better than it was before. This is because, often for the first time, the person is able to relate their memory of the event without going through a fog of painful emotion. He begins to remember details that were previously denied because of their negative impact on his emotional well-being.

Although this is far better than having to talk at length about the past event, for many people even thinking about it is enough to cause immediate upset. If the upset causes the person to break down and cry then you have a situation where the troubled person needs urgent help - and as a TFT therapist you are in a better position than anyone else to give that help - fast! You will have cases where the person will suddenly break down without warning and you have no idea why. But the joy of TFT is that you don't need to know why and still be able to give effective treatment!

Lets look at what you do know. First, under these circumstances you can be virtually 100% certain that your client is reliving a past trauma which has suddenly slipped out from its place under the carpet! Secondly it is not only obvious that the person is thinking about the problem but also that the starting SUD is 10 (or maybe nearer 20 on our 1 - 10 scale)! Thirdly your client is temporarily in no condition to be able to follow your instructions to carry out the treatment.

So this is one of the exceptions to the rule. Normally we sit opposite to our client so that he can copy you while you tap the points on yourself. In this way we can promote the fact that TFT is a very gentle, completely non-invasive therapy. However with your very unhappy client who needs your help quickly, you must tap the person yourself. Start by gently taking one hand and tap the PR spot while quietly explaining: 'I'm just going to tap a few places to help you'. Then carry on tapping the majors while making any soothing sounds as you feel appropriate.

Having tapped the majors, don't attempt to ask for a SUD, but notice that your client will now be a little more relaxed and able to follow your instructions for the 9 gamut.

To keep this as simple as possible, take one hand so you do the continuous tapping on the gamut spot. Then following your instruction you will find your client able to do the eye movements and humming and counting. Finally repeat the majors by your again tapping on the person yourself. By now your lovely client will be giving you a wet smile with thanks and showing a very relaxed state indicating the lifting of a great weight! If that should not happen and he is still showing much distress, then suspect a switch of thought fields to an associated part of the trauma not yet treated and go back to the beginning and repeat the whole process knowing the distress now is the starting SUD of the second thought field. In more complex cases

Thought Field Therapy

this can happen several times - one after the other. (See Case Study - Multiple Traumas and Sticks).

Two important details: You will have noticed I said first take the person's hand and tap the PR spot. This of course is an insurance to be as certain as possible the treatment will work under more extreme conditions where we want the minimum intrusion for the client. From time to time I have some students suggest this would be a good idea for every treatment they give so as to have a quicker success. Yes you could do this - **but don't!** Dr Callahan has explained that if you always do a PR correction at the start of the algorithm as a matter of course, then you will never experience the amazing change in your client due to this simple treatment. One moment your healing progress is totally blocked and after a few taps on the hand, moments later the same sequence gives instant progress! We must never take PR for granted as without the knowledge of how to treat it, our success rate in TFT would be reduced by around 50%!

Next is the trauma algorithm you should use: Complex Trauma with Anger and Guilt.

This is because both anger and guilt are often part of traumatic experiences. You have no idea of the details of your person's trauma therefore include the anger and guilt in case one or other are present. If not a part of the trauma, then TFT will simply ignore the unnecessary tapping points. If on the other hand you don't include guilt and anger, then you could finish up with a person feeling very much better except now feel very angry or guilty! It is far better to resolve the complete problem as a whole.

Lastly we need to look at the make up of the algorithm. By adding anger and guilt to our complex trauma algorithm, we have joined three algorithms together. This is fine and works very well. So you have: eb-e-a-c for trauma, lf-c for anger and if-c for guilt. Put together you have: eb-e-a-**c**-lf-**c**-if-**c** Whereas all those collarbone points will be needed when used with their individual algorithms, they are too many now when put together. **So** use your new effective 'slim version' algorithm which is:

eb-e-a-lf-if-c 9g sq. This will remove the tears and distress very quickly.

5. Case Study and Studies from Students

About eight years ago when Mary and I were inviting people to stay for a weekend of Rest and Healing at our country home Rumwood, on the gentle hills of south east Cambridge, we had a call from a woman in her 50's who I shall call RG wanting to stay for the weekend. It so happened that we had two other women staying also but Mary told me she booked RG to come early on the Friday afternoon because she was certain this person had some problems and was needing help. She felt it would be a good idea to give her a Reiki healing before the others arrived and then a further treatment the following day.

Now a Reiki healing is given with the person lying comfortably on their back on a massage table with head on a pillow and covered with a light blanket. The Reiki is given by gently putting the hands on various parts of the body and often also held just off the body in the person's aura. With soft background music it is a very relaxing and

Thought Field Therapy

soothing process causing most people to be asleep by the end of an hour's treatment.

But for RG it was very different. She lay totally tense and rigid for the whole hour and Mary had never experienced such a reaction before. So she finally asked: "I noticed that you seem to be very tense? " At which RG looked at her and said: "I was waiting to be beaten with sticks" and promptly burst into uncontrollable tears!

Although trained in TFT herself, Mary had not used it much in those days so she called for me to come quickly and help the poor woman.

By the time I reached her RG was still sobbing as if her heart would burst from the enormity of her trauma. As above, I obviously knew nothing of her problem other than it was a major trauma and her SUD by now was around 30! I immediately took her hand and tapped its side to remove any possible PR and then followed through with our excellent 'slimline' algorithm for trauma with anger and guilt. She just managed to cope with the 9 gamut with my help. After completing the algorithm she stopped crying completely - for about ten seconds! ! Then the poor woman suddenly burst out again as painfully as before. So what had happened? She had switched to another associated thought field that also had a starting SUD of around '30'!

I quickly went through the whole sequence again - and again she stopped crying - this time for about 15 seconds - and then once more burst out as if her whole world would break! Realising that this was a major multiple trauma of several different, but associated thought fields, I again took her through the treatment and once more she calmed down completely for a little longer than before.

And so we progressed until finally, after six treatments one after the other, she finally stopped weeping and totally let go all her pent up tension. We could literally see her body collapse as an enormous weight had been lifted from her and she could begin to relax. She got off the massage table, gave us a little wet smile and explained she would like to go and rest. I'm not surprised! ! She was exhausted from her deep sobbing and wailing as well as from the tiring effect of TFT when so much energy is shifted via the meridians and the use of the body's energy.

After her rest by that evening she was fully composed and looking so much better than she had on her arrival earlier in the afternoon.. She now wanted to tell us what it was all about, and quite calmly without the slightest trace of upset, she related a harrowing story of the treatment she received when a small baby and later as a little child. She had literally often been beaten with sticks and half starved when very young! As the weekend progressed she thrived in her new found energy and ability to be relaxed.

A nice little sequel: On the Sunday morning when the others were upstairs with Mary for herbal healing, she came to me and asked if I could help with her pain? It transpired that she had suffered from pain in her back and shoulders for as long as she could remember it. This is the traditional area in the body for carrying the pain of stress and anxiety. So I treated her anxiety of having the pain and then with the pain algorithm while she thought about the pain in her shoulders and back.

After the treatment I asked her how it felt now? Instead of answering, she gave me an excited smile, rolled her shoulders around as if searching for something and then

Thought Field Therapy

said, now with and enormous smile: "It's gone! ! ! My pain had completely gone! ! " And with that she rushed out of the room in great excitement to go and tell the others with Mary.

Why had the pain disappeared so easily? Simply because her body no longer needed it. It had been put in place years ago due to the traumatic stress and emotional pain she suffered from her physical abuse - and now that had suddenly gone - the body was very happy and relieved to let it go.

So poor RG who had suffered so much throughout her life from the terrible traumas experienced when she was very young, was now at last, due to the miracle of TFT, able to lead a normal life unfettered by debilitating flash-backs and physical pain

Case Study - 'Fear of Greens? '

This lady came to stay for a weekend with us and on Friday evening asked me to help her with her fear of greens! Thinking this was a most unusual phobia I promised we would cope with her problem the following day. On the Saturday morning we hadn't been sitting together and discussing her fear (which was a revulsion whenever in the presence of green vegetables) for more than three minutes, when she suddenly burst into tears without the slightest warning! Naturally I hadn't the slightest idea why she was so upset, but I was certain it was nothing to do with greens!

So again we have a situation where we really know nothing, but for a TFT healing we know enough! This amazing ability of TFT to be able to help anyone with any emotional problem without having any knowledge of that problem at all, is I believe, totally unique. And for traumatic stress in particular this ability is a godsend to those suffering such extreme upset and who need resolving help - fast.

So here again we know this poor woman is suffering from a past trauma which has become uppermost in her mind and suddenly overwhelmed her. Her SUD is 10 plus and she's thinking of the problem to the exclusion of everything else - now.

Therefore I took her hand explaining I was just going to tap gently on various places to help her. After tapping side of hand to remove any possible PR block to treatment, I then tapped the majors of our friend Complex Trauma with Anger and Guilt: eb - e - a - lf - if – c 9g sq. At this point - as usually happens - she calmed down a little and was then able to work with me as I took her through the 9 gamut while I was tapping the gamut spot for her. I completed the algorithm by tapping the majors again for her.

By now she had relaxed and gave me thanks with a wet smile. I asked gently whether she would like to tell me what it was all about? But she refused saying she would like to go for a rest. Remember in these circumstances it is usual to shift a lot of energy fast and this will often leave the person feeling very weary. But that's fine! It's one indication of a successful treatment!

Much later that day she wanted to tell us all about her problem: "You see, the reason I'm staying here this weekend is because on Wednesday I have to face the first anniversary of my daughter's suicide! ! Big one! - no wonder she was so upset! She then continued to tell us about her lovely 18 year old daughter who was now lost

Thought Field Therapy

to her and she was able to relate everything quite calmly without any upset at all.

By the time she left she was feeling fairly confident about the actual anniversary on Wednesday but understandably a little apprehensive. I assured her I was at least 90% sure she'd have no trouble, but if she felt the slightest upset, treat herself with the algorithm that I'd given her and had taught her how to use if needed. I also asked her to be sure to ring me if she needed further help and: "Please do let me know how you get on."

Bless her - on the Friday she did ring - and again really wanting to know, I asked how was her day on the anniversary? She said it was the most wonderful experience and she could honestly say that she'd had a happy day! This was because she was now remembering the many wonderful times being with her daughter, doing things together and enjoying the exchange of warmth and love for each other.

She then gave me a brilliant description of experiencing Post Traumatic Stress Disorder - PTSD. She said: "All this past year the terrible experience of suddenly learning of my daughter's death has been like a video - right inside my head and playing over and over again - and I could not get away from it. But now, it's not playing there any more - it's at least three feet to one side and I don't have to look at it - and even if I do it doesn't bother me any more! "

This is such a good description of PDSD because people who have suffered traumatic experiences don't remember them - they play them over and over again as if it was continually happening now. Therefore they cannot get away from it and the debilitating effects can totally destroy their life as they become incapable of normal function because of the insistent video continually playing their past terror or grief.

Another description of PTSD was given to me by a young man after treatment for his past traumas when a small boy. His past problems always occurred in a particular room of their house. After my treatment he was looking back and remembering and for the first time ever he said: "The room is now far away and completely empty." And then he said: "No it's not! It's full of love! "

This reference to being 'far away' is quite usual for anyone who has been suffering PTSD. This is because now that the extreme emotional upset has been removed with TFT - meaning the 'insistent video' has gone - then normal memory takes over and immediately puts the traumatic experience back into the past where it belongs. As previously explained, TFT efficiently removes the perturbation in the thought field from activity and hence the emotional upset disappears. But most importantly, it does nothing to the thought field itself and thus the memory is totally untouched - only the emotion has gone.

Remembering how memory is increased after TFT trauma treatment, and how some people have been told (by the profession) that if a cure is possible it will be because the memory has been eradicated! ! - it reminds me of a time when a young mother came to me for help over her distress from the loss of her child. She was very anxious when she arrived and asked me over and over again to assure her that I would not do anything to her memory. "You see, I don't want to lose my memory of her! ! " Can you believe it? This poor woman was really frightened that I would destroy her memory and so even the one

Thought Field Therapy

thing left to her- the memory of the lost child - would be taken away from her! ! Poor, poor woman, she had been fed such terrible misinformation!

I spent some time gently explaining how TFT would be able to help her and would do absolutely nothing to her memory - except improve it! After treatment was over and she was busily remembering details and telling me all about it, I was then able to remind her how she was now recalling all those details which she had previously forgotten! She left feeling relaxed and reassured.

Remembering the phobia of 'greens,' for interest go to: www.phobialist.com Here you will find around 500 known phobias listed, complete with their Greek/Latin names. The list does not include greens! !

(a). Case Study from student: ' Traumas and Dementia'

J, aged 63 has a sister that lives down the road, M aged 73 who has severe dementia. She lives with H her husband aged 78. H and M have a multi-millionaire daughter who lives abroad. There was a recent event that upset J:

H and M were invited by daughter to go on a day trip with them and for a nice meal. Around midday J receives a call from H with a request to get a bucket of warm water and soap ready. When J puts the bucket next to the front door at H's house, a minibus pulls up with the millionaire daughter, demented M and H together with some other family members. H and M step out off the bus and M is covered from top to toe with faeces - in her hair, on her hands etc.

One of the family members quickly cleaned the bus with the wet cloth and then gave the bucket to J and left her with M and H. Unfortunately H is not capable of looking after his wife anymore. J is very upset seeing her sister in such a state and annoyed because the other family members simply left her to clean up M.

J has had two hip replacements and has to be careful doing any labour. She bathed and cleaned M, washed all the soiled clothes, the house was covered in some places with faeces, she had to clean it up and sort it all out because she couldn't leave her sister in that state.

Problem 1. J described this event as traumatic and afterwards she couldn't sleep, woke up in the night several times, felt angry because daughter with all her money did not, and still doesn't provide a carer/cleaner. J did not want to attend any social functions or go out for a meal.

Problem 2. J felt very awkward confronting the other members on the bus for not sorting the problem out. She is fearful to speak up for herself. She does everything to avoid arguments. After talking to J to discover the cause of this problem, she mentioned an event when she was only six years old. Her mother and J's brother had a huge argument, her brother turned around and wanted to walk off and her mother took the poker out of the fire place and was about to hit her brother on the head. Then her father came into the room and prevented her brother's head being smashed in! J described this event as traumatic and says she sees that 'movie' play over and over again in her head.

Treatment for Problem 1:

Algorithm: Simple Trauma

Baseline SUD: 10 After Majors: 6 After 9-gamut: 5 Treated for PR, After repeat Majors: 3 After 9-gamut: 1 Finished with eye roll. Final SUD 1 After 1 week: SUD 1

J had colour back in her face and she felt very good after treatment. She still felt fine even after a week when she saw M again and she needed a wash but her family still hadn't sorted out a carer/cleaner for M & H. No sign of Apex.

Treatment for Problem 2:

Algorithm: Simple Trauma

Baseline SUD: 9 After Majors: 4 After 9-gamut: 1 Finished with eye roll.

Final SUD 1 After 1 week: SUD 1.

J now told me that the 'movie' had stopped and that this event is nothing more than a distant memory. She feels stronger and has since confronted people about the situation with M. No sign of Apex.

My comment: I'm glad that I was able to help J, she is so much more relaxed at the moment. I must admit she is a 'model' client because the whole treatment went very smoothly. I used your Algorithm recording sheet and Client Detail sheet to document the treatment. I followed the Step by Step TFT Procedure but the treatment was over in a matter of minutes and I was amazed by the speed - especially the trauma from 57 years ago that was linked to the problem of fear and stress in the present. It's really interesting to see how problems are linked to a single traumatic event in the past.

My reply:

What a horrific story J described to you! Poor woman! Thank goodness she had you to treat her with TFT! You were of course absolutely right to treat J with trauma although I think you may have been lucky to have succeeded with just the Simple Trauma algorithm.

If we look at the first scenario you treated, this surely involves several traumatic experiences? Initially the shock of seeing her sister getting off the bus in that terrible state and this then quickly followed by the realisation that no-one was prepared to help her clear up. Then the justifiable anger because rich daughter was not prepared to lift a finger to organise and pay for the much needed help. Further I think she also suffered PTSD over the whole affair and this was causing her loss of sleep as she would be worrying over the issue.

So I think that an initial treatment using complex Trauma with Anger would have been more effective. My guess is that she is still harbouring some anger with daughter although now probably repressed. My feeling is that you have very successfully removed the 'top layer of the onion' which immediately left J feeling able to cope. However there are probably some 'lower layers' still to be addressed.

If you manage to see J again, I suggest you ask her to think of the whole problem again and then ask her if any aspect of it still leaves her feeling upset - then treat that particular thought field.

You did well to find the root cause of J's fear of confrontation and here indeed you had the PTSD which may have linked to the one I've just suggested. Although

Thought Field Therapy

I'm in no way decrying the success you have achieved, I still believe using complex trauma with anger (anger with mother?) and possibly guilt (even as a little girl of six she may feel she should have done more to help her brother?) would have given a more complete treatment. If you have the chance to see her again ask the question: "Is there anything else about that traumatic time which still upsets you now? Are you totally confident when you now have to confront someone over their unreasonable behaviour? " As you say, TFT works at great speed and time in years - or distance - makes no difference to its ability to heal. We are dealing with a 'thought', which having no mass, can travel instantly through time and space. Also the linking of past and present giving the incredible ability to address both associated problems at once. This will frequently happen when you have discovered the root cause - as here which is literally the driving force behind the present difficulties. You will find that most people will be able, even anxious, to tell you about their presenting problems now, but you will then have to search to find the core issues. So often they go back to childhood and once you have treated any core issue, then you are well on the way to solving the total problem. Good work - well done!

Your protocol was exactly right. In problem 1. your PR treatment should be Mini PR when stuck after the 9-gamut - i.e. - the client will need to think of what is still remaining of the problem since at this stage it has already half gone.

(b). Case Study from student: 'Major traffic accident'

R is a thirty year old woman who was involved in a serious traffic accident two years ago. She was jammed in her car after being hit by a lorry and had to be cut out of her vehicle by firemen. She reported at assessment travel anxiety as a passenger and driver, low mood and some visual flashbacks of the incident. She also reported not feeling supported by her employer following the incident or subsequently for her medical treatment for recurrent pain in her neck and back. She is also under some difficulty in her personal life as her partner in unable to find work and so she is the sole wage earner.

During our first two meetings we discussed the accident and the hotspots in her memory which included being cut from the wreckage, the noise of this event and her feeling of panic when on the telephone to emergency services. In more general terms she spoke about the trauma of her father's death when he just collapsed in their garden when she was only 7 years old. She had to call the emergency services then because her mother was out. I had previously introduced R to TFT and we had targeted one of the easier parts of her memory - the sight of an empty motorway before her as she was removed from her vehicle. Her SUDs for this previous thought field had reduced from 5 to 1.

In the most recent session R reported that she was feeling better and that her memory of the whole incident was more distant and not affecting her as much. We agreed to target the part of the memory associated with being on the phone and her sense of vulnerability and panic which she had rated at SUD 8/9 the previous week and now rated as 6/7.

We used the complex trauma algorithm and completed the majors sequence. R reported a drop in SUD to 4/5. This appeared to be ambiguous and since I was unsure

Thought Field Therapy

of the effect of the treatment I took the precaution of using the PR correction before repeating the majors sequence. R then reported 3. We completed the 9-gamut and completed the majors sequence. She then reported SUD 2. We treated for recurring reversal and repeated the majors. R reported a 1 and we finished with the eye roll.

After this R told me of a new thought about the fireman who was trying to make her laugh and how she understood his actions but felt in someway it was inappropriate for her. She identified this as SUD 6/7. We used the complex trauma algorithm and I added the outer eye point for her anger. R reported a sense of her 'tears melting away' but then had a feeling of upset - a dark feeling of being alone, which she rated at SUD 8/9. I was getting the sense of grief and depression and we used the complex sequence which included the sadness point of the eyebrow. After the majors R began speaking about her father dying and her sense of loneliness and vulnerability. We repeated the major sequence without stopping for SUDs as she was clearly distressed. (It may have been useful at this point to have included a PR correction but I did not consider this at the time). R then spoke about her phoning emergency services as a child. We repeated the majors for complex depression. R then remembered trying to call for her mother. This was right at the end of the session and I used the final few minutes to bring her back to the present without attempting to address the issue further. We agreed we would work on the memory of her father's death next time with the assumption that her recent traffic accident triggered some underlying thought fields about vulnerability which had then been re-experienced at the time of the crash and were then reinforced. Although I was unable to get any SUDs for the final stages of this work, the algorithm did seem to help my client access material that she may have been unable to consciously access during the conversation and clearly indicated some unresolved trauma which lay beneath her current difficulties.

My reply:

Indeed an interesting case but I believe not as complicated as it may appear. Basically in TFT terms you have a large 'basketful' of complex traumas. These have inevitably led to PTSD to a greater or lesser extent and they all need addressing in turn to relieve her present upsetting condition. I'm sure your initial discussions over two meetings to access and pinpoint her hotspots of memory was good work from a psychologist's angle, but my TFT mind is saying: "Come on - lets get on with it ASAP and remove the upset from these horrific traumatic memories." Especially as we are aware that these people don't remember the past events so much as re-play them over and over again as if it was still happening now. This is the real distress which TFT can remove more quickly and completely than any other therapy.

So I would have started right at the beginning which I guess would have been the tremendous bang as the lorry hit and the instantaneous change of her world as she wondered initially whether she was still alive!

That would probably be the first thought field to treat with complex trauma plus guilt and anger because you never know when these can so easily pop up. Then move on rapidly to the next thought field - eg. being totally alone for a while before any help arrived and realising that she's trapped - then next, maybe the panic of being on the phone to emergency services followed by noise

Thought Field Therapy

of being cut from the wreckage etc. etc. Just following from one thought field to the next in quick succession as they are brought up by the client. In this way you can shift an enormous amount of emotional upset even if the person is very distressed by the memories - don't worry because any extreme upset will last only for a very short time. In these cases don't bother with SUDS and indeed use side of hand for PR correction first before each treatment. So you will treat trauma after trauma until the client shows a major relaxation because all the emotion is now removed.

I may be exaggerating this case because I'm not sure whether R may have used some coping techniques during the intervening two years and so her reactions now are not so extreme. However, treating the traumas in turn still applies although you will be able to discuss and get SUDS accordingly. Your treatment of her panic on the phone was fine until you arrived at SUD 2 - do remember that just a simple eye roll is all it takes to bring it down to 1. After this you got going nicely following R as she began coming up with thought field after thought field.

Your future plans with R sound excellent. Moving to release her past traumas of father's death and her vulnerabilities etc. will now be to the forefront of her mind because the upset of the accident and all that involves has been removed first. However I'm wondering whether you gave her at least the trauma algorithm to use on her own at home if and when further aspects come into her mind? This self treatment between visits can often make an enormous difference to the overall success of a client's problems and your being able to attain a complete and final resolution of all the parts that make up the complete picture. After this any psychological treatment to help her move forward with her life will be invaluable.

7. Grief

1. What is Grief?
2. Treatment for Bereavement
3. Treatment for Divorce or Separation

1. What is Grief?

Most of us will have our answer to this question since it's not possible to go through life without experiencing times of grief to a greater or lesser extent. The loss of someone or something of great importance to us. Usually this is the death of someone we love which causes great grief. Also the loss of a beloved animal such as a dog or horse which has been a part of our lives for many years. Death is of course inevitable and very often expected. But sudden death due to an accident is very different and can cause enormous grief. Separation or divorce although quite different can have a similarity in that it could involve the 'loss' of a loved person.

In some cases the grief will be short-term and this is a normal human emotional response and during the grieving process we can learn to accommodate the loss and get on with our lives. Therapeutic intervention is rarely needed and may indeed be particularly unwelcome.

Nevertheless, how well we manage that grief can have a major impact on our quality of life.

Unmanaged grief can lead to chronic post-traumatic stress and, if it continues to remain unresolved, may develop into post-traumatic stress disorder.

We use the term "bereavement" to define the response to the death of a loved one yet it is only one form of grief. The common emotional pattern of bereavement is easy for others to understand and empathise with. However, if that pattern is mirrored when the grief arises from incidents not involving death, such as divorce, then that understanding and empathy is reduced and may even not be present at all! This loss of support, which can be real or imagined can speed progression into psychological disorder, especially for children.

2. Treatment for Bereavement

Initially, your bereaved person is likely to be in a state of shock and numbness, even when a death has been anticipated. They may feel faint, cry uncontrollably, become hysterical or even collapse. Sometimes you will see the opposite and the person displays no emotion at all, appearing very controlled, calm and detached. You will find this response more often from men. Unfortunately, it can be misinterpreted by partners and others as cold-hearted and callous, which only adds to the isolation and stress the poor person feels.

This initial pattern may last several days and usually allows the bereaved person to deal with immediate necessities and cope with, for example, the funeral without losing control. The emotional responses will vary and draw

Thought Field Therapy

heavily on cultural expectations, traditions and rituals. They must be respected. No-one is going to come to harm or have their quality of life destroyed in the short term and it is prudent not to offer therapy at this time, unless it is specifically requested.

Over the following weeks or months most adults and children gradually restore their lives to what would be regarded as normal. Assistance with emotional turmoil is most welcome during this time and this is where Thought Field Therapy comes into its own. Teaching the bereaved person the Complex Trauma algorithm (eb - e - a -c 9g sq.) plus Psychological Reversal corrections to help themselves at any time, is a tremendous boon. Apart from its ability to resolve traumatic stress in a few minutes, it is also uniquely empowering. Your bereaved person now knows he can help himself and so doesn't need to visit their Doctor for medication, consult a Counsellor for hours of talk, nor suffer the well-intentioned but ill-informed ministrations of friends. So the bereaved person is essentially back in control of day to day events.

Of the few who fail to cope with the death of a loved one and remain in a state of traumatic stress, more involved intervention is required. It is not possible to go into as much detail as I might wish and I recommend that practitioners research the various manifestations of grief in adults and children (and its normal progression) very thoroughly before attempting therapy. However in most cases TFT can have considerable success if the following emotions are taken into account:

Anger and Frustration - very common in cases of sudden death (heart attack, stroke, etc.) or fatal accident. The bereaved seeks to blame someone or something for the loss of their loved one, yet cannot successfully rationalise that blame. Physicians who attempted to save the deceased's life often bear the brunt of this anger, with partners coming a close second (compounded, if the partner is male, by the bereavement response discussed above).

Use Complex Trauma + Anger algorithm (eb - e - a - c - lf - c 9g sq.)

Guilt - the bereaved person may feel that they have failed the deceased loved one in some way. The manifestations of this are too numerous to mention, but usually revolve around past untruths which are now not admitted, perceptions of not having cared enough, or imagining having contributed to the loved one's death in some way. In a therapeutic situation, it is wise to get to the bottom of all of the bereaved person's perceptions and treat each issue of guilt individually.

Use Complex Trauma + Guilt algorithm (eb - e - a - c - if - c 9g sq.)

Depression, Disorganisation and Despair - Here bereaved people have failed to make progress in the resolution of their grief, and have considerable difficulty planning future activities, even from minute to minute. This is characterised by lack of concentration and focus, procrastination, fear of the future and unwillingness to seek help.

Use Complex Trauma + Depression algorithm (eb - e - a - c - g50 - c 9g sq.)

Withholding - the bereaved person here does not discuss their loss in any way, as to do so causes considerable emotional pain. This can be a very frustrating experience

Thought Field Therapy

for this person because he has a deep but unresolved need to recall the happy and joyful times and to discuss their loved one's life, while other people are often expecting and demanding this. So Instead, the bereaved isolate themselves from their friends and family so they will not be obliged to do so.

Use Complex Trauma + Depression algorithm (eb - e - a - c - g50 - c - 9g - sq)

Do be aware that offering treatment may be met with considerable anxiety as the bereaved is concerned that the therapy may make them "forget" about their loved one. This fear is often made worse during conventional therapy, as counsellors often encourage bereaved people to develop new interests and meet new people to "take their mind off their feelings". Once again, TFT comes into its own as these people can be reassured that only the emotional pain and suffering will go, and that all their memories will remain unaltered. Also remember to remind them that their memory of the deceased loved person will actually improve since now they are remembering without any emotional pain, they will find themselves remembering little details it was not possible to access before your treatment. You can emphasise how TFT can lead to immense liberation as it's now possible to think of the deceased person as often as he wishes and talk to family and friends without any upset whatsoever.

3. Treatment for Divorce or Separation

Divorce or separation can have considerably more impact on a person's emotional well-being than a loved one's death as the object of their affection or disaffection remains within reach. Essentially there is no finality to the relationship. All of the emotions discussed above are magnified and becoming traumatised over and over again is common if complete isolation from the former partner is not achieved.

Sadly, adults are very adept at discovering ways of managing their own grief in such situations but surprisingly ignorant of their poor children's needs. Most children, even when a parent has been abusive towards them do not "take sides" in a separation or divorce. But they miss the absent parent as much as if he or she were deceased.

As with bereavement, children of junior school age may experience similar feelings to adults, such as separation anxiety, confusion, anger and guilt. They may not show their feelings openly, leading parents and others to believe that they aren't affected by the traumatic events. Common behaviour changes include becoming withdrawn, bed-wetting, lack of concentration, clinging, bullying, telling lies and being aggressive, all of which may indicate their upset state.

Teenagers' grief reactions are similar to those of adults but negative feelings may lead to violence and aggression. Mood swings and periods of depression are common but it may be difficult to separate them from normal adolescent behaviour. Tension and fighting within the family can become more common. Like adults, teenagers may also suffer from headaches, sleep difficulties and eating disturbances.

TFT intervention remains the same no matter what the origin of the grief or other symptoms.

However, a word of caution when treating children:

They often unconsciously develop multiple minor emotional problems which serve to cover over a major trauma in their lives. TFT intervention will usually be very successful in eliminating those uppermost problems. Unfortunately, just like taking the lid off a pressure cooker, the major problem will then reach the surface. So watch out for this because if the child is not in a controlled, supervised environment or place of safety the negative consequences for an unprepared therapist and the child itself could be considerable.

8. Anger & Rage

1. What is the Difference?
2. Understanding Anger & Rage
3. Treating Anger and Rage
4. Case Study

1. What is the Difference?

It is most important to know which you are dealing with as the TFT Algorithm for Anger is quite different to the one for treating Rage. And you don't want to get it wrong do you? - because we all know what happens - nothing! ! TFT can be so protective in this way.

So - Definition: <u>Anger</u> can be regarded as an emotional state accompanying irritation or frustration that does not extend to physical violence against objects or persons and that can usually be controlled by act of will.

<u>Rage</u>, although arising in anger, is a much more severe emotional state that often extends to physical violence against objects or persons and can rarely be controlled by act of will. It is therefore characterised by loss of emotional control.

2. Understanding Anger & Rage

We all get angry from time to time, but usually the mild to moderate sort! However do remember that anger is a very powerful emotion which although not escalating into the physical damage of rage, can nevertheless cause great and lasting emotional damage. Lets have a look at some very likely areas where anger causes so much damage:

- Damage to relationships - personal, social and in business,
- Interference in judgement and decline in performance,
- Non-compliance with accepted norms and rules,
- Engagement in unsafe and dangerous behaviour, including criminality.

Rage is a more 'dangerous animal' because the individual sees no way out of an irritating or frustrating situation due to a perceived loss of status or ability to influence the outcome. The desire to bring the triggering circumstances to an immediate end by any means becomes overwhelming.

3. Treating Anger and Rage

It is vitally important to say that a therapist should not agree to treat a client for anger or rage problems unless they are both are in a place of control and safety. This would usually require a supervised environment and immediate availability of help should it be necessary.

However it is more than likely that you will meet clients who have mild to moderate anger associated with issues such as anxiety, trauma, intimidation (as in bullying at work), depression and so on. So as always, be sure to question your client carefully to ensure you discover any anger that may be a part of the problem you are treating.

Remember when treating trauma, for example, both anger and/or guilt are often a very visible part of the traumatic stress experience, but be aware that anger may also be covert, as a component of any other presenting condition.

For example, guilt can also be treated as "anger directed at oneself", and depression can be treated as "repressed anger". Anger treatment should almost always be included in the approach to problems such as relationship issues, performance enhancement, bullying or intimidation, etc. Remember you don't just take a 'quick statement of the problem'! ! A comprehensive history taking is always vital to reveal the thought fields where the anger algorithm is needed.

IMPORTANT! Never try to treat rage 'live' - you won't succeed! ! The person in a rage is far more likely to lash out at you and would certainly not listen to anything you were saying! But you could certainly treat your person's rage when he is purely thinking of the situation that causes the rage to erupt.

For example, suppose the client suffered from Road Rage. He could be asked to imagine situations on the

Thought Field Therapy

road where he just 'loses it' and you treat with your rage algorithm while the client is imagining being in the car right now. Of course, the outcome cannot be tested until the client encounters the real life situation again, but hopefully your excellent treatment will prevent any further problems since you now have a serene person who is no longer fazed by the 'odd traffic difficulty'! !

4. Case Study

HS, a Muslim of Yemen descent, suffered from migraines. He was very obviously tense most of the time and was given to making rude, cruel and abusive comments. I suggested to him that I could help him by means of TFT and that there would be no charge. HS accepted the offer.

I asked HS what he considered his biggest trouble to be and he said he didn't know and then asked me what I thought his problem to be. I then asked him if he ever felt troubled by irrational anger. HS then admitted that he often had great anger accompanied by extremely violent fantasies towards Americans, Jews and people he considered to be foolish, weak and stupid.

Since he has so far been able to prevent his anger becoming action, we tried the anger algorithm first. I asked him to think of George Bush and then give me a SUD. HS reported a 10 accompanied by graphic descriptions of various acts of mutilation to be applied to the aforementioned president. Then asking HS to keep in mind the object of his hatred, I guided him through the anger majors. The following SUD was a 3.

HS immediately seemed to be somewhat sleepy in appearance and uncoordinated.

The 9g was then performed and the second set of majors with my assistance due to his lack of coordination. I then asked HS how he felt about George Bush out of 10 and he replied that he loved the man and if he were sat here now he would shake his hand!

I then asked him how he felt about the weak and the stupid and the SUD was 8. We went through the anger algorithm again and the SUD was reduced to 1 by the end of the sequence without the need to correct for PR. By this time HS was barely able to keep his eyes open or stay upright on his chair, so I concluded the session.

Myreply:

What could I say? !

Anger triggers the body's "Fight or Flight" response - powerful activity of the sympathetic nervous system and the release of adrenalin gets us ready for action. We feel very roused, ready to fight if the need arises; our heart rate and blood glucose concentration rises to give us the "get up and go"; our faces go pale as blood is diverted to muscles that will drive us on.

HS had these rapidly restored to minimal activity with TFT and almost certainly had the sympathetic activity replaced with that of the parasympathetic - "Rest and Digest". We feel languid and relaxed, our heart rate falls and our "get up and go" gets up and heads off to bed...

No wonder HS felt so accepting and sleepy!

9. Phobias

1. What is a Phobia?
2. Understanding Phobias and Traditional Treatments
3. Treating Phobias
4. Treating Phobias associated with Past Trauma
5. Case Studies

1. What is a phobia?

A phobia is an irrational fear which is triggered by a specific, yet objectively harmless, object or situation. The fear response may be initiated by either the actual or anticipated presence of that object or situation in the sufferer's immediate environment. The consequent state of anxiety varies from mild to profound panic, but is always unreasonable or excessive.

Almost invariably, the sufferer will agree with an observer that the object of their phobia is harmless yet will insist that they cannot control their response to it. This usually leads to strict avoidance of the object or situation, or the adoption of coping strategies to manage the anxiety and stress their phobia brings about. As one might expect, such strategies can have profound affects on the sufferer's personal, social and work life.

It is important to understand that the fear experienced by the phobic is in all respects normal. It is the triggering factor of the fear response, or the intensity of that response, that is abnormal. The phobic, for whatever reason, considers the object of their phobia to be a threat to their well-being or even their life. Just as a non-phobic would be fearful of a genuinely life-threatening situation, the phobic is essentially giving the same response.

Treatment is therefore focussed on breaking the inappropriate link between perception and response.

2. Understanding Phobias and Traditional Treatments

We all know these fears are unreasonable and irrational but we must remember that they are very real and truly terrifying to the phobic person. Also we need to remember that these people only experience great fear *when in the presence of whatever causes their fear.* At all other times they are completely normal and display no upset. For many however, the mere thought of being in the presence of their fear is enough to cause considerable upset.

Many people who do not suffer any phobic fears do not understand the phobic's genuine fear purely because they do not experience it themselves and so do not understand why this person is 'making such a fuss over nothing'! This can cause them to be quite vicious in their attitude to the unfortunate person and, for example, demand to know: "Why do you have to mess up everyone's holiday just because you won't go on an aeroplane? You know perfectly well that it's the safest form of travel! " Or again for example: "Why can't you come with us on that delightful coastal walk along the top of the cliffs? " These attacks are very unfair and cause enormous distress for the phobic person especially as he knows the fear is totally irrational and this knowledge adds humility to the suffering.

Some traditional ways of treating phobias is enough to make your hair stand on end! There is something called **counter conditioning** where the person is trained to substitute a relaxation response for the fear response in the presence of the phobic stimulus. The idea is that relaxation is incompatible with feeling fearful or having anxiety, so it is said that the relaxation response counters the fear response.

This process is sometimes extended to be a more gentle process by very gradually introducing the feared stimulus in a step-by-step fashion known as **systematic desensitization**.

However the technique I find the most horrific is called **exposure technique**. It seems that the perpetrators of this 'therapy' believe that by forcibly making the phobic become immersed in his fear somehow the fear itself fades away! !

Frankly in my book such a treatment should be made illegal. Yes, if the person actually makes the decision to face his fear, then I have no problem with that and admire his courage. But to force the poor person must be wrong? And what about their 'uman rites'? ! !

As always our TFT treatment for phobias is dramatically different! Often the one quick treatment taking just minutes is all that's needed completely to remove any phobic fear and your client will immediately be able to face their previous fear without the slightest trace of any upset - that is if you get it right from the start!

It is essential to know if you are really dealing with a true phobia or with a past traumatic experience.

3. Treating Phobias

Start your treatment by asking: "How long have you had this fear? " If the answer is: "I'm not really sure - most of my life I believe" and "I remember my mother telling me I used to be afraid of....when I was a young child." This establishes that you are dealing with a true phobia which is a Neotenous Fear. Neotenous is a biological term meaning 'lack of complete development'. We have learnt how these phobic fears were put in place in the infant child as a protection for the species and were later, as the child gained some maturity and hence understanding, subsumed naturally by nature. For those whom this 'natural TFT' did not take place, the adult is then left with the full phobic reaction and so we must do nature's job - albeit a little on the late side! !

Remember how a new born baby has no awareness of height or any other danger because it can do nothing other than just lie in its crib - and hopefully not cry too much! But as it becomes a little older - around six months - it begins to crawl and so, for the first time in its life, becomes aware of a changing perspective due to its own movements. At this point nature immediately introduces the phobic fear of heights to protect the child. The lovely experiment to prove this was done by putting a collection of little people with their be-nappied bottoms on the floor at one end of a largish room. All the mummies were crouched at the other end of the room calling to their offspring and encouraging them to crawl across for a loving cuddle. In the middle of the floor was a large portion which had been removed and replaced with thick strong clear glass through which could be seen a deep drop. Not one of the busily crawling babies went over the glass - they all perceived it as frightening and crawled around it!

By the age of 1½ to 2 years old nature will have done her work and the phobic fear will be gone, leaving only the normal understanding of the danger involved when in a high place. This was shown to me many years ago when my daughter was just 2½ and I was busy building on to my house with the help of a local joiner. We were working at first floor level and had put up scaffolding with planks and ladders to erect the walls around the floor already in place. Soon after completing these preparations one afternoon, a small voice behind me asked: "Please may I come up daddy's big tower? " Phobic fear obviously did not exist for her but my immediate reaction was to refuse because 'it would be too dangerous for her etc.' Then I quickly realised that to refuse would probably put her in greater danger because she might climb up when I wasn't present. So I said: "Yes darling of course you can, but first you must learn how to climb a ladder" So I went up tight behind her telling her how to hold each rung and then how to come down backwards and so on. Very soon she was going up and down with plenty of ability on her own and running around on the large floor area. No, she did not run off the edge! She kept well away from the edges because she knew quite naturally that the edges represented danger. Nature does indeed look after its children! She would then go up and down while Tony and I were working and I was totally confident then in allowing her to do this because she knew what to do and remained safe. I would just keep an eye on her from time to time because familiarity can breed contempt and that is when the accident can happen.

Recently, my daughter who is now 44 years old, told me she remembers that incident when she was a little girl and how grateful she was at the time that I put my trust in her and allowed her to climb the ladder to my 'big tower'. It shows how easily as a parent we can, without thinking, dismiss a reasonable request from our children due to our own perceived fear. This in turn can then so easily lead to a resentment in your child becoming established as a permanent distress.

So having established your client does have a true phobia, treat it with the phobia algorithm and after checking that the SUD is definitely down to 1, then and only then, you can suggest to your ex-phobic that he might like to be exposed to the cause of the previous fear. You will then know for certain that your treatment has been totally successful when your client enthusiastically agrees to go and look for a spider, or climb up your steps to be well above the ground. If you're like me and don't have a handy 757 on your lawn waiting for take off, then the experience of flying has to wait until arriving at the airport on the next planned trip. Also be sure to remember that the algorithm for Spiders, Turbulence or Claustrophobia is different from the 'standard' treatment. Yes, it is just a variation on a theme: a-e-c 9g sq. instead of the usual e-a-c 9g sq. but it literally makes the difference between success or failure.

Thought Field Therapy

If ever proof was needed to show that the correct sequence is vital to TFT, it was revealed to me some years ago when treating a young woman for her great fear of spiders. She was one of those extreme cases where she would only enter a room after 'casing the joint' by looking around the top of the wall and the ceiling to be sure of no lurking spider minding its own business! It was an afternoon when I was being careless! We discussed her problem, explained TFT and started at SUD 10 or higher! "Please tap under your eye, and under your arm and then your collarbone. How great is your fear now?" I asked, full of confidence. "It's still about 10 or more" she said. Oh well never mind and I asked her to tap side of hand and repeat the majors. When asked she again told me it was as bad as before and sounded rather sad. So off we go and I instructed her how to rub the sore spot and again repeat the majors. How now? But no, she assured me there was still no improvement at all! I was then thinking this is unusual for a simple phobia - surely we don't have a toxin problem? So have you spotted the 'deliberate mistake?'

As for Hercule Poirot, Agatha Christie's famous Belgian detective, "Now at last - the little grey cells - they are working!"

Quite casually (so as not to give my shame away!) I now asked my client: "Please will you tap under your arm, under your eye and your collarbone." Immediately without any hesitation she said: "Oh, that's better, it's now a 7." We then completed the algorithm without any problems and quickly finished at SUD 1 and total reassurance from her that she would be happy to come with me into my workshop where we might find a spider! This is where SOD's law took over and a spider was not to be found but she literally poked her fingers into the cobwebs during her search!

Yes, sequence in TFT does matter!

4. Treating Phobias Associated with Past Trauma

Now for the different treatment: On your initial enquiry "How long have you had this fear? " if the answer is: "Well about X years, before that I used to have no trouble at all." So you enquire what happened X years ago? (For example) "I was enjoying the view from the top of a church tower and the crowd behind me accidently pushed so hard that I nearly fell off to the ground far below. I was only saved by someone grabbing my legs just in time! I was never afraid of heights before then."

So here we are dealing with an Atavistic Fear, meaning a normally subsumed fear has been reintroduced into the thought field (usually by a traumatic experience) and so causing the full return of the fear. This is quite different from the true phobia and must be dealt with accordingly. So your treatment must be to address the cause of the person's present fear by taking your client back to the actual traumatic happening, imagine he is experiencing it again now, get the initial SUD and treat with complex Trauma - adding anger and/or guilt if either should be relevant. Once the effect of the trauma has been resolved, the present fear will also disappear in many cases as there is now no driving force to feed it. For others who are still aware of some fearful feelings if thinking of being in the situation, treat their fears with the normal fear algorithm, remembering as always that there might be some associated thought fields also needing to be resolved.

Fear of Flying is a common phobia which can often be due to a trauma: "Oh, I used to fly all over the world on business, no trouble at all, but now! - I can't even reach the airport without becoming terrified." OK, so what happened? Discover that the client was involved in a crash-landing X years ago (or last month, it makes no difference to your TFT treatment) and of course ever since then has been terrified of aeroplanes. The trauma of his experience is the cause of his present fear and so you treat with complex trauma while he imagines being in the crash now. Then check any present fears remaining and treat as needed.

Initially most people will enquire: "Can you cure my fear of flying? " The answer is basically Yes, but you need to take time to discover exactly what the person really means as it's a blanket description which embraces a range of different fears and therefore different thought fields. So start by asking: "What are you afraid will happen to you if you fly in an aeroplane? " In a few cases the answer will be that the person is afraid that the wings will fall off or the engines stop and they will fall to the ground and be killed. Treat this thought with the fear algorithm unless on questioning you find that the client really panics over such an idea becoming reality for him - in which case use one of the panic algorithms. As always, watch out for switching thought fields to associated fears. Treat each as they come up.

More often you will find the client targets a specific part of flying. For example: "I'm fine until the stewardess shuts the door after we're all sitting down. Then I feel trapped and out of control." Claustrophobia! So take your fearful person to that very moment when the door has just been shut, get a SUD and treat the claustrophobia.

Other examples are people who 'manage' all right until they realise that the plane is now revving its engines at the beginning of the runway, the brakes are let off and the airport buildings are whizzing by at great speed and your person is now terrified they will never leave the ground and are about to have a terrible crash! Again have your client imagining being in the speeding aircraft now, get a SUD and treat with the fear algorithm or a panic treatment if this seems appropriate.

One more typical example is the client who maintains that she is not really afraid of flying but does experience great fear when the aircraft starts bucking about the sky and the captain advises they are hitting a patch of bad weather and seat belts must be put on. Turbulence! No problem, take your client to the bucking plane now, have her imagine it really heaving around - even feel it doing this! - and you will get a high SUD! Use your algorithm for Turbulence, remembering always that together with Spiders and Claustrophobia, it must be treated with the alternative sequence:

a-e-c 9g sq. After treatment always look for any other fears associated with flying that the client hasn't mentioned to you - possibly because the one you have treated is always uppermost in the person's mind to the extent that it may block lesser fears from her awareness until you ask about it. It is this sort of research on your part which can give a complete treatment so you finish with a happy client who now has no fears or worries at all = job well done!

Thought Field Therapy

5. Case Study and Studies from Students

'The would-be Pilot'

CB is a 43-year-old woman who had recently trained with me in TFT Algorithms.

She contacted me because she had decided to live in Canada and was totally terrified of the flight.

She explained that her fear was so great that even arriving at the check-in would cause a panic and she would immediately run away! If she ever managed to screw up enough courage to get past check-in, she would have the same overwhelming panic when waiting at the gate and would certainly run away.

On further questioning, I discovered that 15 years ago she was sitting in a plane waiting until everyone had boarded for a trip to the UK. Suddenly she was completely overwhelmed with total panic and literally ran off the aircraft! Ever since then she has not been able to fly. I realised this was almost certainly the core issue causing her present problems. Treating this was complicated by toxins (Wheat, Sugar, Chocolate and Red Meat) which had to be treated first and then two diagnosed sequences to bring this past trauma down to SUD 1.

CB, feeling more relaxed, now realised that she had been putting the traumatic fear of 15 years ago onto her present flight and was therefore scared that the same thing would happen. We treated the fear of being in the check-in queue at her flight to Canada in five days time. This dropped to a 1 with another dx sequence. Then the same sequence quickly removed her panic feelings of being overwhelmed while at the gate. At this stage she was very relaxed and happy. I asked if there was any other aspect of flying which still frightened her - take off, landing, turbulence etc?

"No" she said, "that's fine, **you see I'm not afraid of flying at all. If I can afford it, I want to take my Private Pilots Licence and learn to fly a small aircraft!**

She left looking forward to her trip to Canada and feeling confident she would not experience any trouble at all.

Some poor people who are terrified of flying but haven't yet found the powerful healing of TFT will spend hundreds of pounds on desensitisation programmes sometimes run by airlines . They are taught the basics of how an airplane flies and why it won't fall down to the ground and kill them. And then, irrespective of their present fears, they are all put in an airliner and taken for a trip round the airport and back. This is meant to prove to them that everything they've learnt works perfectly and so now they have no fear at all! ! ? 'Well yes actually, I'm just as frightened as I was before this flight and now I'm so glad it's over'! ! 'Flying? No not for me - it's far too dangerous'! !

Case Study - 'The Vancouver Trip'

Some years ago when I was still giving Traditional Thai Healing Massage as well as TFT, one of my regular clients rang me on a Tuesday afternoon in a mini panic: 'Robin I've got to fly to Vancouver on Thursday morning and **I'm terrified of flying - can you help me? !** ' I said 'You better come over to-morrow morning and I'll see what I can do.' After ringing off I thought there's nothing like leaving it till the last minute!

When she arrived I quickly discovered that she was one of those 'white knuckle' people who is so afraid of

Thought Field Therapy

everything that she will continually grip the arm of the seat so tightly that the knuckles go white. Horrible airline food? Forget it - how can you eat anything when you have to grip the seat?

I gave her fear treatments for her various intense fears with several aspects of flying including her feelings of claustrophobia when the stewardess shuts the door after everyone has boarded. Although every thought field started at SUD 10 each time she thought about being on her plane to Vancouver, after treatment all was down to a 1 and she said that she was now feeling much more confident and although a little apprehensive felt she would be able to manage the flight.

And that would have been that for me as I heard nothing from her and I had now lost contact. However a full six months later she suddenly popped up on the phone asking whether I could give her a Thai Massage as she was now back in Cambridge!

After explaining how good it was to hear from her after all this time, I asked - really wanting to know -' How did you get on with your flight to Vancouver? There was a short pause while she was organising her memory and then she said: "Oh that trip! It was amazing! " She said: "When I arrived at the airport I found I was not feeling afraid and later we had to wait at the gate for about half-an-hour. Normally I would be sitting and gripping my chair with white knuckles, but to my amazement I was able to sit back and enjoy reading my book."

She continued: "When we were all on the plane and settled in our seats I still found to my great surprise that I had no fear at all. I was so amazed that I told the stewardess all about it and the stewardess was so amazed that she told the captain all about it and the captain was so amazed that he called her onto the flight deck to join them and watch the let-down and landing." (This was before regulations put in place after 9/11).

Finally she told me that watching the landing take place with the runway gently coming up to meet them for a perfect landing was almost 'a spiritual experience' and 'One of the most wonderful happenings in her life! '

(a). Case Study from student: 'The holiday balcony'

This lady has a problem with heights, not being able to go near or even close to elevated areas. Knowing that the client was going on holiday it was likely that the apartment would be on a level higher than 2. So I prepared my client with a list of algorithms to help with the anticipated problem. This was how the situation unfolded:

On arriving at the holiday resort and getting the key for her apartment, she found she was on floor 9! Just the thought of getting in the lift to the 9th floor caused her problems. As she got into the lift she started to do the PR all the way to the 9th floor, then getting into the apartment only to find there were patio doors in the front of the lounge area and main bedroom leading out to a very small balcony and then straight down!

She went into the bedroom and asked her husband to leave her. She then started doing the phobia algorithms e-a-c- 9g sq. As the phobic fear was at its most extreme at that point her SUD was 10. When the algorithms were completed she felt it was down to 2 and so you can imagine her husband's surprise when she called him into the bedroom and he found her standing on the balcony

Thought Field Therapy

enjoying the view! For the rest of the holiday there were no further problems with heights.

My reply:

A delightful little 'vignette' for this person with a very good result due to her own efforts! I believe you were very lucky to have a client who faithfully followed your treatment instructions when on her own - unless of course you already know her and knew she could be trusted to work with you in this way?

Personally I would have treated her myself first while she was thinking about standing on a balcony and brought her down to a SUD 1. Then sending her away with the algorithm to use on herself **if** needed - which may well have not been necessary. Also treating her yourself first would have proved that you were dealing with a true phobia and not addressing a fear engendered from a past traumatic experience. Certainly a great experience for her - and her husband! It should bring more clients to you as she relates her story to friends!

(b). Case Study from student: 'The holiday travel and wasps'

My client is a 56 year old female who has suffered from low self esteem, lack of confidence and general anxiety for many years. She is very anxious about walking alone anywhere or travelling on busses, even well known routes. I have worked on this client for 12 years giving Indian Head Massage, Reflexology, Hypnotherapy and Personal Development. She has improved over the years but fundamentally is still very anxious and frequently feels out of control.

TFT Treatment was agreed to in respect of travel to Poland with her family for a holiday which was a huge challenge and her first trip abroad. I had already tried hypnotherapy and TFT for this. She also wanted to try TFT for her fear of wasps and claustrophobia in lifts. There were no specific memories relating to any of her symptoms but all seemed to have been there since childhood. It was after the holiday this client then told me she had only undertaken TFT to please me as she trusted me - but didn't think it would work!

Fear of travel: Initial SUD 10

Simple phobia fear - I chose this algorithm as it appeared to be a straightforward fear caused by anything out of her comfort zone.

e-a-c tapping majors: SUD 8

9 gamut, repeat majors: SUD 5

9 gamut, repeat majors: SUD 3

9 gamut, repeat majors: SUD 3 As there was no further reduction used Mini PR, first level - as this is the first time it was needed to reduce SUD. SUD now 2

EYE Roll: SUD 1

No identifiable toxins present.

Client did Apex by saying it was very difficult to think of the problem especially as she was having to concentrate on the technique. She had suffered this problem for a long time and was used to this feeling - it was hard to think about it for long, even though before the treatment she was saying she was feeling panicky every time she thought about the journey and everything she was about

Thought Field Therapy

to undertake. I was surprised how easily she responded to this treatment as I had expected it to be more complicated.

After the holiday she commented how amazed she was at the treatment's effectiveness and that it's magic! Her family were amazed too at her staying calm throughout the lengthy and delayed car journey. Her son commented he couldn't believe how calm she remained while even his Polish wife got more upset with delays etc. She even went to the local restaurant on the campsite on her own to try the local food for breakfast whilst the others ate in the cabin. Impressive indeed in a strange country!

Fear of wasps: Initial SUD 10 - the closer the wasp gets the more anxious she feels. She has always been afraid of them. Simple phobia/fear algorithm used.

Majors: SUD 8

9 gamut, repeat majors: SUD 6

9 gamut, repeat majors: SUD 3

9 gamut, repeat majors: SUD 1

Eye roll.

Straightforward treatment, no PR corrections required. The client felt very tired and wanted to sleep after the session.

After the holiday she reported that there were an unbelievable number of wasps in Poland but she remained calm and thought: "Well it's just a wasp and it will go away" whilst her son was flapping around with newspapers etc. He said he couldn't believe how calm she was! The whole family were really impressed by her reaction again and my client told me how happy she was with the effects of TFT. We also tried the same sequence for her fear of lifts but this hasn't been tested yet.

My reply:

Your choice of the phobia/fear algorithm for the first treatment (travelling to Poland) is fine and you started well reducing the initial SUD 10 to 8 after the majors. So far so very good. But then you went into repeat mode treating with the 9g and majors three times in a row! ! Yes, using this process you managed to 'hack your way down' to SUD 3 and then - at last! - the 'little grey cells, they were working' and you used the Mini PR correction and immediately you were able to conclude the algorithm satisfactorily!

Do you remember how I told you never to repeat something that is not working? So you see in this case, after your reduction from SUD 10 to 8 with the majors, your next step of 9g and repeat majors left you at 5. At this point the algorithm is finished and you are still at 5. Therefore before you start anything else you must think - there is a problem and what is the required treatment now to overcome it. Since you have already progressed to 5, you are looking at the need for a Mini PR correction to address the PR now present in the remaining part of the upset. This you did correctly but not until you had repeated all those 9g/repeat majors first! After the PR correction, the SUD would have immediately reduced to 2 after just repeating the majors. Your eye roll after that was perfect and you arrived at a SUD 1

In future I do suggest that you always get the SUD immediately after the 9g before carrying on with the repeat majors to complete the algorithm. This is because you will find cases (unlike this one) where the SUD does not reduce after the 9g. Therefore you use a PR correction at this point which saves you having unnecessarily to do the repeat of majors before discovering the hold up. Remember that you must always go right back to the beginning of an algorithm after any PR correction and start again. A good example of Apex! "It's difficult to think about - or - "I can't think about the problem" always means a SUD 1. Well done!

Your treatment for her fear of wasps was fine but, of course the same remarks about repetition apply as before. I think a very likely result would have been:

SUD 10 Majors 8

9 gamut 6

Repeat majors 3 or 2

Finally either treat 3 with Mini PR and repeat just the majors = SUD 1

OR treat 2 with eye roll = SUD 1

Her final amazement of the effectiveness of TFT showed her logical brain had had enough time to understand and accept the treatment!

Your remark about fear of lifts and using 'the same sequence' would be ineffective.

Remember this is claustrophobia, and together with the fear of spiders and turbulence, these three need the alternative algorithm: a-e-c 9g sq.

Excellent results!

10. Substance Addictions & Obsessive Compulsive Personality Disorders

1. **Presentation**
2. **First contact with your client**
3. **Treatment of urge/desire to indulge**
4. **Psychological Reversal and the addictive force.**
5. **Addressing both sides of the problem**
6. **Further treatments to combat the addiction**
7. **Case Studies**

1. Presentation

What makes an addict? A simple question that is not easy to answer because we all have habits and/or preferences that are part of our personality. For example, this can be reflected in a desire for tidiness in the home. Untidiness can lead to you feeling anxious which you then relieve by the simple act of tidying up! But is this an addiction? The answer lies in examining whether or not an individual's quality of life is affected by his or her actions. We would probably agree that your quality of life is affected if you consume a substance that is known to be harmful to your health, or have an uncontrollable urge to re-arrange your friends furniture to your own satisfaction whilst on a social visit!

In terms of substance addiction, Charles Roper (1998)[7] defined the following categories and signs that are a very useful guide for the TFT practitioner:

The Social User: One who uses simply to enhance the pleasure of normally pleasurable situations. The social user experiences the following:

- No negative consequences;
- No surprises or unpredictability;
- No loss of control;
- No complaints;
- No thoughts of or need for limit setting.

The Substance Abuser: One who uses to enhance pleasure and/or compensate for something negative, such as physical or emotional pain, insecurity, fear, anger, etc. The substance abuser experiences some or all of the following:

- Occasional negative consequences that are not repeated;
- Promises that are made and kept;
- Complaints are heard and dealt with.
- Limit setting that is adhered to;

The Substance Addict: One who uses to celebrate or compensate - or for any other reason, legitimate or not.

---
[7] Charles Roper (1998): http://www.alcoholanddrugabuse.com

The addict experiences four or more of the following over a consecutive 12 month period, with varying degrees of severity:

- Negative consequences are recycled;
- Complaints are denied and/or not heard;
- Limit setting and promises to self or others are broken;
- Reliable symptoms of addictive disease become more evident as the person's addiction is established:
- Continued use despite negative consequences;
- Using more of the substance than had been anticipated.
- Repeated efforts to cut back or stop the substance use.
- A reduction in social, occupational or recreational activities in favour of further substance use.
- Loss of control, as in more use than planned (broken limits);
- Unpredictability, as in use despite stated plan not to use (broken promises);
- Compulsivity/preoccupation in thinking;
- Denial and use of defences to maintain denial;

Thought Field Therapy

- Remorse and guilt about use or behaviour when using;

- Memory loss, mental confusion, irrational thinking;

- Family history of addictive behaviour;

- The development of tolerance to the chemical in question.

- Withdrawal discomfort (physical, mental, emotional, and/or psychological).

- Use of the chemical to avoid or control withdrawal symptoms.

- Intoxication at inappropriate times (such as at work), or when withdrawal interferes with daily functioning (such as when hangover makes person too sick to go to work).

Here we see a considerable 'basket full' of problems that make up the profile of a typical addict! The practitioner's decision whether or not to commence treatment essentially begins at the level of the Substance Abuser, the level at which addiction can be said to begin.

So where would those with Obsessive Compulsive Personality Disorders (OCD / OCPDs) fit in? In the realm of TFT, OCPDs are regarded as addictions to patterns of behaviour rather than to a substance. Whereas one person might be addicted to a chemical - nicotine in tobacco, alcohol, heroin, etc. - the other is equally addicted to a habit or thought - excessive hand-washing, nail biting, continuous worries and anxieties over insignificant matters, to name but a few.

As addiction to a behaviour can be less well defined here are additional significant signs to help you. The individual may be:

- absorbed with details, lists, order, organisation, rules or schedules to such an extent that the original purpose of the activity is lost ("can't see the forest for the trees");

- a perfectionist to such an extent that the perfectionism interferes with the completion of the task;

- overly dedicated to work, to the extent of exclusion of leisure activities or quality time with partner and children.

- overly conscientious, inflexible or scrupulous about ethics, morals or values out of keeping with cultural or religious influence;

- a hoarder, saving worthless items of no real or sentimental value;

- uncooperative or will not delegate tasks unless others agree to do things the way the individual insists.

- stingy or miserly toward self and others;

- unduly rigid and/or stubborn.

In short, preoccupation with direct control, orderliness and perfection dominate the individual's life to the detriment of efficiency, flexibility and openness.

There is one final and very useful distinction:

Thought Field Therapy

Obsessive: The individual has a constant desire to carry out action or thought - indulgence does not bring the desire to an end at any time.

Compulsive: The individual has a constant desire to carry out action or thought - indulgence brings the desire to an end at that time.

For example, as already mentioned, the compulsion to spring clean one's home can be considered perfectly acceptable as completion of the task ends the compulsion - until next time! However, if completion of the task doesn't end the compulsion and the spring clean continues unnecessarily and exceeds what a reasonable outside observer considers acceptable, then the individual has entered the realm of the obsessive.

2. First contact with your client

These problems of addiction is one of the few where we are not able to resolve the issue immediately, such that the client can go home after treatment without their addiction any more. This is because we have to combat the powerful addictive force which is busily ensuring the person 'stays addicted'!

So when you are first contacted by the addict - let's say they are a smoker - who invariably asks: "Can you stop me smoking? ", your answer needs to be: "No I can't, but you can." You should then qualify this by explaining that you can show the addict how to resolve his problem within a few weeks with just a few minutes effort each day during that time.

Go on to emphasise that if he follows your simple instructions exactly, then his problem will most likely be gone - and, of course, if your addict doesn't comply then you can promise that his problem will certainly remain!

If your addict now shows the slightest hesitation, then the best advice is to say to him that: "At the moment I don't think you are really quite ready to give up. It's best that we end our sessions now as you'll only be wasting your time and money if we continue".

Why so harsh? Simple. You can be quite certain that these people will not treat themselves every day to keep themselves out of psychological reversal and will therefore not address their urge to indulge as it arises - result: continued addiction!

This moderate threat of "take-away" may help your addict fall on the positive side of the fence they've been sitting on. If so, reiterate what you've just said to be absolutely sure they want to continue voluntarily.

Let's now assume your addict gets over this first hurdle, often because he has tried everything else and is now desperate. We'll also go on assuming that we are dealing with a smoker for the moment (since these are the ones you are most likely to encounter).[8] As you make the appointment for their first visit, ask your smoker to be sure to arrive really needing to have a cigarette.

This is very important as you need to start his treatment by quickly removing the desire to smoke. If you forget to arrange this, you can be sure your smoker will have a

---

[8] In the practice of TFT, the same procedures apply to every addiction, chemical or behavioural.

quick last drag in the car before coming in to see you and so will no longer have the urge to indulge at all!

3. Treatment of urge/desire to indulge

As usual, obtain a SUD from your smoker by asking "On a scale of 0/1 to 10, how nice would it be to have a cigarette right now? " If the smoker has their cigarettes with them, you could have them place an unlit cigarette between their lips to force the pace. More often than not they'll reply with a figure between 8 and 10. Now you should quickly take the person through the first of the addiction algorithms whilst they continue thinking of their need to have that cigarette. If that doesn't work, continue through the alternatives.

What are we waiting for? Easy, the common response from your smoker when asked how much they'd like a cigarette now: "Well, at the moment I don't seem to want a cigarette at all! "

Let's enter their mind - what are they thinking? "Wow! This is weird! What's going on here? This therapist has taken away my need for a cigarette - that's brilliant! ! Hey, what else does this person know? "

In other words you have immediately impressed your addict because you have done for this person the very thing he has always been trying to do himself - remove the need to smoke. So now this needy person is much more likely to listen seriously to everything else you have to explain.

4. Psychological Reversal and the addictive force

Now I want to put a dividing line right down the middle of this problem called Addiction. One side I'm going to call "Desire - the urge to indulge". The other side, "Addiction".

So far we've been working only on the desire, the need to indulge, and how to remove it. You have found your client is very happy when you say: "I'll now show you how to remove your need to smoke every time you want a cigarette". But now lets encourage him even more by saying: "I'll also show you how you can help yourself never to need another cigarette again! "

Here's an interesting phenomenon - now ask how this idea grabs your client and the reaction will usually be: "Oh! Ah! Um, I'm not so sure about that" - he will resist because he cannot accept the possibility of never having another cigarette!

You have deliberately crossed my dividing line with your addict and addressed the addiction head on! There is a very powerful force at work here and it's essential you understand the principle behind it:

All addicts are psychologically reversed in relation to their addiction.

As you know, a person in PR sabotages their own healing. You cannot resolve a problem for someone in PR. The actions taken will be the opposite of the thoughts. The addict will therefore do the opposite of what's wanted - that is continue to indulge rather than stop smoking. The addictive force is very strong and takes away the choice

Thought Field Therapy

of whether to smoke or not - indulgence always wins! In other words, having successfully had the urge removed their motivation even then prompts them to say: "*I will still give this up but I'll have one more for the road first*".

But, as Roger Callahan says, no-one is reversed for giving up the addictive urge because they consume their chosen substance (or carry out a behaviour pattern) to eliminate the urge anyway. If they were reversed for addictive urge then their motivation would be directed to achieve the opposite, i.e. **NOT** consume the substance, carry out the behaviour, etc.

So, you must treat both sides of your addict's problem simultaneously if you are to achieve total resolution.

5. Addressing both sides of the problem

On the side of Desire - the urge to indulge, you must teach your addict always to remove the need by using one of the addiction algorithms. This treatment is done every time there is a desire - but not otherwise.

On the other side, the Addictive Force, your addict must keep himself out of PR by tapping the PR spot on the side of the hand every waking hour. Also he must do the Collarbone Breathing exercise three times a day to keep out of Neurological Disorganisation. These treatments must be done every day *irrespective* of whether there is any desire to indulge or not.

This is the moment when your addict probably decides you are quite mad! "How can I be expected to tap my hand every hour? What's going to happen to my life? "

You ask your person to think of what needs doing in his workplace and explain:

"When you arrive at your place of work in the morning you have a hundred tasks to address which leaves no time for fiddling about tapping - correct? " Well NO!

What am I really asking you to do? Tap-Tap-Tap-Tap-Tap, it's a two or three second job!. You can even use the edge of a desk, a steering wheel, the arm of a chair, the spine of a book, or whatever comes to hand, to do the tapping for you! "

"What about when you think - 'I really must send that email to X' - Oh! Tap-tap-tap-tap-tap - now I'll send the email; I need to make that urgent phone call - Oh! Tap-tap-tap-tap-tap - now I'll make the call'"

"So you see it's so quick and simple it won't affect your life at all - and it can be done in public because no-one will really notice! "

Finding a time and place to do Collarbone Breathing is rather different. Here we can empathise with our addict! "Imagine if you're sitting at your desk puffing in and out and tapping yourself at the same time and your boss or workmates happen to spot you! - They're likely to think 'Poor old soul - a very good employee all these years but now...'"

So advise them to do collarbone breathing in the morning before leaving for work, in the evening on arriving home and again last thing before bed.

You must endeavour to send your addict away still not wanting a cigarette. If his urge has returned simply treat the urge again. Once again, emphasise that it's vital he

Thought Field Therapy

taps the side of the hand every waking hour every day and perform collarbone breathing three times a day.

You can also explain that the process works because each treatment of the desire removes a different level of the underlying anxiety, that driving force behind the desire to indulge. The evidence of this happening is clearly shown, because every time the algorithm is successfully used, the desire is removed and the addict is aware he no longer needs to indulge.

Also you must explain to your client that if he has, say, 50 levels of underlying anxiety that trigger the urge, then it will obviously be necessary to retreat it 50 times before the total underlying anxiety will have gone! Once this has been achieved the demand to be satisfied will also have gone- and the person will become fully aware that there is no longer any need - or desire - to indulge any more.

Finally, empower your addict to help himself. Emphasise that he now has the ability and the tools to resolve his own addiction, BUT it is completely up to him. He must follow your guidance to the letter, and the problem will, in the vast majority of cases, be solved.

Remind him that the success of the treatment relies on full co-operation. If this falters, he will quickly slip back into PR and will not then treat the urge as it arises. The addictive force will take over and the choice not to smoke will again be lost.

Be very sure your addict comes back for a second visit as soon as possible, but certainly within a week. It is vital to check on his progress (or otherwise!) and if necessary 'read the riot act' because you are having to battle a very strong force doing its best to sabotage any attempts to neuter it.

6. Further treatments to combat the addiction

So, we can now see very clearly that resolving someone's addiction is not a simple case of: "Here, grab a quick TFT algorithm, get rid of your desire, throw away the cigarettes, bottle, drugs, etc. = job done!! No, we have to make a determined effort to address the many problems involved in a complex network of thought fields together with the co-operation of the addict who must understand that working *with* you for a period of time is essential if he is to be free of the habit.

Mats Uldal TFTdx, from Norway, has found that it is much easier to help anyone to halt an addiction if you first find out what anxieties the person has about the thought of actually quitting. These fears are very real to your addict and are often many and varied:

- fear of losing a "friend",
- fear of losing social skills,
- fear of being the only non-addict amongst addict friends, i.e. being left out or feeling alone,
- fear of gaining weight,
- fear of coping with social pressures to indulge,
- fear of losing the "the reward",

Thought Field Therapy

- fear of losing a simple method to relax,
- fear of having a "new life" to get used to...

- and so on. Now TFT can be used to get rid of all these fears by using the appropriate algorithms while the person thinks of each of their anxieties in turn. Unlike the underlying anxiety causing the continual desire, these problems are very specific and so can usually be removed completely with each treatment. When this has been done the client often has a greater will to succeed because no irrational anxieties intervene to ruin his or her willpower.

Here's a useful tip: emphasise to your "addicts" that TFT will not *make* them stop their addiction but will give them back the *choice* not to indulge. In other words, before your treatment they feel the urge to indulge in their chosen substance or pattern of behaviour and they have the choice - "do I indulge or do I not indulge? " Of course, the substance / pattern of behaviour wins the argument, and the wrong choice is compulsively made.

After successful TFT the *same* choice is there - except this time it's a **genuine** choice - the substance / pattern of behaviour does not automatically win.

However, if the wrong choice is still made even though there is *no urge* to indulge, then they are self-sabotaging - and you can do nothing further for them until their PR-based self-sabotage is corrected. As we know this is properly done by the client tapping Side of Hand <u>every hour</u>, <u>every day</u> whether there is any urge to indulge or not.

For substance addicts (tobacco, heroin, etc.) there is the added problem of toxin overload - almost every substance addict's "barrel" of toxins is full to the brim. It takes time for the level to fall once they are not adding to it every day. Hence, in the early stages, if another toxin is encountered (e.g. a chemical in coffee) it can temporarily fill the barrel to overflowing and the urge treatment is undone. This is why it is vital that the person repeats the algorithm as soon as even the slightest urge appears. The signs for toxin involvement include the client saying something like "the urge is greatest whenever I have a cup of coffee". In this case the coffee probably contains a toxin that triggers the anxiety that manifests itself as the craving or addictive urge.

It's worth bearing in mind that many addicts also have great difficulty in visualising themselves as non-addicts, or not indulging in pressure-laden situations. So use the Visualisation Technique.

If for example he is a smoker, take him to the point where there is a visualisation of happily smoking and then switch it to imagining never having another cigarette - ever! This will be impossible for most smokers, so get a SUD for the difficulty in imagining the desired state where a SUD of 10 means it's literally impossible to think of such a result. Then treat it with a-c-9g-sq. Your addict will look puzzled and agree that he can now imagine the real possibility of never smoking again.

Another problem is "apex-based" and is the most common reason for people not attending follow-up sessions. The client didn't believe that the successful reduction of their addictive urge was due to the TFT treatment and so doesn't repeat it as instructed. This needs a bit of cognitive readjustment! Here's what I use, assuming the client has returned for a "booster"...

"Have you ever taken something like aspirin or paracetamol tablets for headache? " [YES]

"Do they get rid of your headache most of the time? " [YES]

"Do you understand how the tablets work to get rid of your headache? " [NO].

*"So even though you don't know **how** they work you know for certain that they do? "* [YES]

"How do you know that it works? " [WHEN I TAKE THE TABLETS THE HEADACHE GOES AWAY]

"If I told you to take a headache remedy to get rid of a headache but you didn't follow my instructions, would you expect your headache to go away? [NO]

*"Well, TFT treatment is just like that. You **know** it works because you told me yourself that your addictive urge went down to 0 after we used it last time. You don't understand how it works, of course, but it did. If you choose not to use something that you know works for you, then your problem will be just as bad as ever, and I can really do little to change that."*

I also have a compliance test for those who telephone for help or return for their booster. I take them through the first set of majors of a holon and then say *"I've just got to write that down, could you do the 9 gamut procedure yourself, please? "* Those that have complied with the self-help requirement will, of course, be able to do this as they will have done it many times! You'll hear them hum and count in the background.

However, there are those that will then give a long pause then say "what's that? ". Those clients get a further stern chat about following advice!

The special case of Smokers...

Smokers will make up the greatest number of addicts a typical TFT practitioner will see. Unfortunately, they can be the most obstinate!

Many will have tried to give up smoking before, multiple times in some cases, and failed. They will also expect you to work a miracle - without making any effort at all themselves. "I will give you the moon if you can get me off the fags" an inveterate smoker once said to me. "Fine" I said, "Come and see me", knowing perfectly well that he would not come - and he didn't! This needs challenging.

Before I treat a smoker I usually have an "adult to child" transactional chat about their smoking habit, its dangers and risks, not only to themselves but to their partners, children, etc. Some practitioners recommend that you have the client imagine the worst case scenarios of what their life / health / well-being will be like 1 year from now, 5 years from now, 10 years from now, and so on, if they continue to smoke. Take them through a full, detailed visualisation of this.

There are then two possible tracks to follow as well as urge reduction with TFT.

Reinforcement by aversion: The smoker is reminded about such things as the stale odour they carry, bad breath, being anti-social, etc. Subtle psychological "tricks" can also be played:

- **Guilt:** asking the client (who has young children) to imagine a point in the future where he is still smoking and has just been diagnosed with terminal lung cancer. Now ask him to imagine how he will break this news to his children - to tell them that Mum or Dad is leaving them, never to return.

- **Jealousy:** asking the client (who has a good relationship with her partner) to imagine the same scenario, but remind her that, after her own death, her partner is hardly likely to remain faithful and celibate.

- **Disgust:** "Have you ever wondered about the conditions those who pick tobacco leaves work under? 16 or more hours a day with no breaks because every leaf they pick earns them a little more to add to their already very meagre pay. Now, if they have no breaks what do you think they do when they need to relieve themselves? Easy - they do it where they stand. And remember there's no toilet tissue in a tobacco field so the next best thing has to suffice. And do you honestly think that they're then going to throw away something that could earn them a little more cash..? "

Reinforcement by positive imagery: The smoker is reminded of the health and lifestyle benefits that will come from giving up smoking. Albert Belling TFTdx from Chicago has said that he helps his patients make their reasons to quit as personal and specific as possible. "For my health" is impersonal and non-specific; "to be able to keep up my energy when I'm playing with my grandchildren" is both personal and specific

Why are these "extras" needed at all?

The main reason for using other strategies in combination with TFT is that TFT gets rid of the urge to smoke but not necessarily the learned "habit" which has been conditioned into place in a Pavlovian fashion over many years. Most often, the TFT reduction in the anxiety-linked urge is enough to overcome the habit but some people need a bit more "inner strength" to do it.

This conditioned response is often the cause of what I call "false failures" - I get a client calling me up because they say the TFT has failed. I ask if the urge is still as strong and they reply "Oh, I have no real desire to smoke but I smoke anyway." The TFT had worked, it was just their conditioned reflex to smoke in certain situations that needed knocking out

In addition, if I get a hint that the client may just fall into habit rather than urge, I suggest that they put their cigarettes out of reach so they have thinking time to consider using TFT, or that they give the pack of cigarettes to their partner to be "handed over" only after TFT has been done and even then only if this fails to eliminate the urge.

In any follow-up session I remain a devotee of the stern "adult-child" transaction with those who won't make the effort. I would want to know the exact reason why, when they have the evidence of their own response, they do not use the tool they're given. If the answer is "can't be bothered" or "I'm a bit embarrassed to use it" or any similar excuse then I give them a good talking to about

Thought Field Therapy

wasting my time. You need to choose who you use this on very carefully, of course! For me this has had quite an impact on occasion because I'm effectively playing "take-away" with them and the threat of losing the chance to quit concentrates their mind! Once they're well and truly into the "child" mode I can then force the pace toward achieving the goal of "non-smoker"

So good luck with your smoker and don't be discouraged if you don't immediately have complete success. It is a rocky path for you as the practitioner but, as always, you will have more success the more practise you have and get better at helping these people. Your rewards can be great when receiving genuine heartfelt thanks for your life changing help.

7. Case Study and Studies from Students

SK is a young man of 30 years old who presented with a severe case of obsessive hand washing and the need to make continuous checks on everything from whether a door is locked, the oven turned off, and that everything, especially ornaments, are properly in their place.

He had previously undergone Cognitive Behavioural Therapy and Counselling to try and ease his problem which was now completely controlling his life. Neither therapy had helped at all, but rather tended to make matters worse for him.

I decided to start by trying to find out why he had this problem which had been with him for many years and was now, he told me, becoming worse. After considerable questioning, he finally explained that when he was only a small boy of five or six, he was continually frightened and traumatised by his parents who were always rowing with each other and who would become extremely angry with him if he interfered with various articles and ornaments around the house. He had a younger brother and so he had to keep checking that his brother also had not moved any ornaments before his father came in because he was very frightened of his father's anger.

Starting with his trauma as a small boy when parents were arguing, he gave a SUD 10 which quickly came down to a 4 by using Complex Trauma with Anger and Guilt Algorithm.

He then switched thought field to his extreme fear of his father finding ornaments out of place. This again was SUD 10 which very quickly came down to 1 using the Complex Trauma Algorithm.

He then told me of the time when he was 21 years old and in his first year at university. His parents had had a major row and he was very traumatised by this. Starting at SUD 9 this also was cleared with Trauma, Anger and Guilt Algorithms.

When SK arrived, I noticed he continued to wear his cap in the house. Very many years ago my father would have been extremely offended by someone doing such a thing in his house! Times have changed - and I took little notice of this. Now, however, he took it off to reveal a large bald patch on the front of his head. He explained he had literally caused this himself by pulling and rubbing his hair and was very ashamed, embarrassed and anxious about it.

His SUD for this was 10 but immediately came down to 1 by using the combined Algorithms of Anxiety, Anger,

Thought Field Therapy

Embarrassment and Shame. It must have taken a full 20 seconds to resolve this problem!

When my wife, Mary, came in to meet him later, he took off his cap to show her and prove his total lack of upset.

Finally, I addressed his endless hand washing. His need to wash was now at SUD 10 and this was, as always, treated with the Anxiety Algorithm. Again at great speed he came down to 1 and then sat looking bewildered and looking for Apex explanations!

He then volunteered to touch the floor with his hand - something he could never have brought himself to do before without immediately rushing to wash his hands. After doing so, I asked whether he now needed to wash, and he said "No, why bother"? ! !

I sent him away very happy and aware of being truly relaxed for the first time in as long as he could remember. He touched the floor once more because he wanted to and did not wash his hands the whole time he was with me.

I had given him the full OCD treatment to continue at home with instructions to see me again in two weeks for a check on progress. He rang me at that time to cancel the appointment explaining that he had completely stopped hand washing within four days and all other obsessive and compulsive habits had disappeared. His old traumas caused no problems and he was happy to talk about them since there was no upset at all. He told me he "would have travelled to the moon and back" to get rid of his obsessions!

I think this is yet another case which shows not only the truly awesome power of the Callahan Techniques TFT completely to resolve a long-held problem, but also how important it is to look for possible core issues which are driving the presenting problems. This man's considerable suffering was being literally driven by his past traumatic experiences.

Unlike most OCD's and Addictions, there was not a major invasive underlying anxiety which continually needed to be repressed by the tranquilliser (cigarette, hand washing etc.) but rather specific and powerful traumas, the emotional impact of which demanded frequently to be subdued. Remove these past traumas completely, as we do with TFT, and equally immediately any need to repress the upset has disappeared.

(a). Case Study from student: 'The occasional smoker'

'Client B was an occupation manager and a smoker who, over the years, had managed to cut down but could not reduce the four a day she continually needed. She mentioned that she is the sort of person who is generally quite relaxed and calm and that it takes a lot to stress her out.

I therefore felt that as there appeared to be no underlying issues, algorithm 4 for addictive urges would be beneficial. This was done at a time when my client was due to have a cigarette.

Initial SUD was 9 for her need to smoke.

Tapped the majors and the SUD was 2

9-gamut sequence = 0 (Did not tap majors again as at 0, was that right)?

Eye-roll.

Thought Field Therapy

Client reported not wanting a cigarette and appeared relaxed following the session. Has since reported that she does the tapping throughout the day at the times she used to have a cigarette and she has not had one since.

I feel that this client entered into this therapy with an open mind and a positive attitude and has found it to be very easy to slot into her daily life when needed and is delighted with the results.'

My reply:

Well done! However we can look at some improvements for use in the future. Firstly, right algorithm for the problem and you were absolutely correct in not 'hacking on' with the sq. just because it's there when it's obviously not needed. In this case we could have taken the principle further! You started perfectly with the great need to indulge and after the majors only, there you were at SUD 2! ! No further treatment needed - just finish with our friend the eye roll! Do you remember when I took you all through some sample treatments, the second one was just this - straight down from a 10 to SUD 2 after the majors only? And I promised all of you that you would experience this amazing thing happening? The only thing I did not promise was that it would happen so soon as it has for you! !

Since your client was already smoking so few a day, the addictive urge would not have been very strong. So leaving her with only the treatment to remove the urge whenever it arose was adequate and indeed seems to have cured her problem. However for the average addict smoking 20 or more a day, this treatment would not have been enough since you were not treating the addiction. So do remember in future, you will normally have to make sure your client is also tapping PR spot (side of hand) every hour and doing collarbone breathing (cb2) three times a day. This is essential to make sure the client stays out of permanent PR and also addresses her neurological disorganisation. Without this she will not treat himself for the urge to indulge and the treatment will be a failure.

11. Depression

1. What is Depression?
2. Treating Depression
3. TFT Treatment for Depression

1. What is Depression?

Quite often my clients come to me and on asking about their problem I'm told: " I'm depressed!" Then I ask: "Who told you that?" Invariably the answer is : "The doctor and he put me on anti-depressants!" "Did they help you?" "No not really – maybe for a short time!"

There's a general impression that anti-depressants – Selective Serotonin Reuptake Inhibitors (SSRIs) more often than not – have been handed out over recent years like sweeties! This could indeed be the case but remember that conventional medicine has little else to offer. Sadly, there are many given such pills who experience little or no long term benefit.

Does this mean that they weren't suffering from depression in the first place? A difficult question to answer as depression can be a 'blanket term' that covers a multitude of sins!

So what is depression? Well, I believe we all have our own answer having almost certainly suffered from its effects sometime during our lives to a greater or lesser extent. Have a look at this list of mood characteristics which are used clinically to determine if a state of depression is present:

- Being unable to gain pleasure from activities that normally would be pleasurable.
- Losing interest in normal activities, hobbies and everyday life.
- Feeling fatigued and having no energy.
- Insomnia or waking early in the morning.
- Having a poor appetite, no interest in food, weight loss.
- "Comfort eating" - having an increased appetite, weight gain.
- Losing interest in sex.
- Difficulty in maintaining focus or concentration.
- Feeling restless, tense and anxious.
- Irritability.
- Diminished self-confidence and self-esteem.
- Avoidance of social contact.
- Indecisiveness.
- Feeling useless and inadequate.
- Feeling hopeless and despondent.

- Thoughts of self-harm including suicide.

Haven't we all experienced three or more of these signs & symptoms at the same time? Arguably, very few people will escape episodes of depression at some time during their life. In fact we can reasonably say that depressed mood is a normal human reaction to many of life's challenges.

This mood we feel takes us out of the triggering situation temporarily and gives us the opportunity to take stock and re-examine 'what is going on here?' In most cases the episode resolves itself very quickly with no lasting effects – other than an increase in our wisdom! Depression in these cases is not of much clinical significance and its complete resolution can found through passage of time or the judicious use of TFT.

However when the depressive mood continues beyond two weeks without any improvement and there is even an increase in severity and number of symptoms, then we could be looking at clinical depression.

2. Treating Depression

Here we have to be very careful and remember that most of us are not medically trained. If clinical depression is a confirmed diagnosis, it is essential at this stage to ensure that the sufferer is under qualified medical supervision. You should ask your client to confirm that he has sought advice and / or treatment from his GP, essentially as a safeguard against the client getting worse and claiming that you, as a complementary medical practitioner, were negligent in some way.

Also do ensure that the patient does not stop taking any medication prescribed by their GP. If such medication is stopped abruptly, a sudden decline in mood or increase in severity of symptoms (including suicidal thoughts) may well result.

If TFT treatment has a positive outcome, then the patient should consult their GP before making any reduction in their medication.

Furthermore, as a practitioner you have a duty of care to ensure that the patient is in a safe place in case the treatment does not have the desired outcome. Supervision after treatment is always advisable - possibly by a friend or relative or access to immediate advice.

3. TFT Treatment for Depression

If in doubt – DON'T TREAT but refer to the GP. Yes, I know we have assured practitioners that TFT cannot do any harm even if you get it totally wrong – all that then happens is nothing - the client is no better or worse off.

However, it's all too easy to provide the client with TFT treatment only later to have the treatment fail or, if initially successful, have it undone by toxins. How will the client then react?

Do remember that it is very usual for these clients to be toxic to their medications and this will either limit the impact of TFT treatment or undo a treatment after a while.

But I'm not saying don't treat depression at all! If you are satisfied your client is in the care of his/her GP - and you have advised him / her very clearly that any decline

Thought Field Therapy

in mood is to be discussed with that GP first - then by all means go ahead and help your person with your TFT algorithm for depression.

It is also important to be sure you are truly dealing with depression. There are many other conditions - stress, anxiety, guilt, anger, trauma to name just a few - that are accompanied by depressed mood.

Have another look at the list above and you will see that many of the symptoms can indeed be due to actual depression, but in many cases can also be present for totally different reasons. It is not unlikely that your client is suffering from a 'basket full' of problems which together will cause him to feel depressed. So, as always, it is good practice to seek out the root cause of these feelings and treat them in turn.

A typical case would be your client worrying about, and being very anxious over, "this and that", whilst also fearing "the other" and even suffering a trauma over something else! Put together in the person's 'basket full' it can bring on feelings of depression.

Simply treating for depression only will not solve this problem. We have to address each aspect of the total problem on the onion layer principle and only expect resolution after all thought fields have been treated. Where have we heard all this before? Why, stress of course! Your stressed person weighed down under a blizzard of daily problems is often reduced to a depressed state. Remove each cause of the overall problem called stress and the 'depression' will disappear.

Remember to take care and do not be tempted to go beyond your abilities when helping depressed people.

They need help and lots of it, so if you are genuinely sure of your abilities, help as much as you feel able and good luck !

Finally, a little quirk of English usage. The Advertising Standards Authority will not allow any advertising from non-medically qualified persons if it includes claims to treat "depression". This is to help ensure that the first port of call for someone seeking treatment for depression is their GP. Quite right. However, those who engage in complementary medical treatment can claim to offer treatment for "depressed mood".

12. Physical Pain

1. What is Pain?
2. Treating Physical Pain

1. What is Pain?

You don't know? ! ! I don't believe you! Unfortunately we all have to suffer it at times and - TFT can sometimes help. The International Association for the Study of Pain defines pain as: 'An unpleasant sensory and emotional experience associated with actual or potential tissue damage or described in terms of such damage.'

However, it is important to distinguish between acute and chronic pain as their characteristics differ considerably.

Acute pain

This usually results from:

- disease
- injury to body tissues
- inflammation

Acute pain also has a sudden onset and may immediately be accompanied by anxiety or emotional distress. The cause can usually be identified readily and managed appropriately. It has an essential role in warning the sufferer of immediate damage being caused to the body and in forcing the sufferer to limit activities that might delay repair of the damage.

The period of time over which the pain is present and its degree of severity will vary in relation to the nature and extent of the cause, but is always self-limiting.

Chronic Pain

Chronic pain can be regarded as a disease in itself, beginning either as acute pain or having a much more gradual onset with no readily identifiable cause. The pain persists over long periods of time, sometimes in the absence of apparent injury or inflammation.

Environmental and psychological factors play a part. Cold, for example, can cause or exacerbate joint pain, and anticipatory anxiety about feeling pain can lead to increase in its eventual severity.

2. Treating Physical Pain

First consider the appropriateness of the pain.

Acute pain is appropriate, e.g. it is warning of damage occurring or having occurred to the body and serves a purpose in preventing the sufferer from engaging in activities which trigger the pain. This allows for the body's natural healing processes to operate without hindrance.

Chronic pain may cause unpleasant sensations to be present in the complete absence of immediate damage. Similarly, chronic pain may also be idiopathic (a disease, but of unknown origin), there being no recognisable causative factor. In other words, pain is definitely present but is inappropriate as it is not serving a warning purpose.

As an example, consider the experience of someone suffering from chronic arthritis. When they move their affected joints, the eroded ends of the bones rub against each other causing further damage to the surface. Acute pain is the result and is appropriate - it is warning of damage occurring at that time and forces the sufferer to stop moving the joint.

Later, the sufferer may be sitting quietly in a chair, or lying in bed, when the same joint begins to ache severely with no provocation. No damage is being caused as the joint is not moving, yet pain is clearly being felt. In this circumstance the pain is inappropriate - it is warning of nothing, other than any inflammation that may be present.

TFT will have little or no effect on appropriate pain. Treatment cannot subvert the body's all important warning signal. Nevertheless, where the pain is so traumatising that psychological factors are increasing the degree of pain perception, TFT treatment can bring about a reduction in its severity.

TFT is particularly effective with inappropriate pain. The mind appears to allow its removal as the warning signal is simply not required.

So for many people you will find the anxiety or fear of having the pain can be successfully treated with TFT first whether you are addressing appropriate or inappropriate pain. After resolving this distress, then you can move to addressing any inappropriate pain where this is present - usually with success.

For a dramatic result in treating physical pain look at chapter 6 on Trauma and refer to the sequel at the end of the Case Study 'Multiple Traumas and Sticks.'

A cautionary note

The grin-and-bear-it attitude of a significant number of people (males and the elderly of both sexes in most instances) underreport or ignore pain. For this reason it is essential to ensure that your client has consulted their GP before any pain treatment is undertaken. **The experience of pain is to be taken as a warning of underlying pathology until investigation proves otherwise.** Only when medical investigation has identified the cause, or eliminated potential causes, should the practitioner offer treatment.

13. Therapy with Children

1. The Legal Issues.

It has always been a laudable aim within TFT to "take it to the children". There is no doubt whatsoever that children's lives could be transformed if they had regular access to TFT, especially if it could be used within schools.

UK children, however, are now probably the most legally protected on the planet. Unfortunately, it also means that a lot of things that would be so useful for them to know or learn are held back from them for fear of litigation.

This is no bad thing, of course. As there is no statutory regulation of Complementary Medicine in the UK, anyone can set up as a therapist - no previous experience or qualifications required - and without any vetting of suitability or character.

A number of high profile child-abuse cases brought the inadequacy of the law concerning those working with children into sharp relief and the response was immediate.

The Protection of Children Act 1999 (PoCA) made it a statutory requirement that Child Care Organisations (defined as any organisation that provide accommodation, social services or healthcare to children), the NHS and other Independent Healthcare Organisations, consult the PoCA List and List 99 (individuals barred from working directly with children on misconduct or medical grounds) before offering employment to an individual, either on a paid or voluntary basis, if that employment meant that the individual came into regular contact with children in the course of their duties.

Groups such as the Scouts, Guides, Youth Clubs, etc., were also given the entitlement to consult those lists, but not the mandatory duty to do so. Most, however, do.

Effectively, anyone who wants to work with children with any of the above must have had a Criminal Records Bureau (or north of the border, Disclosure Scotland) check carried out. In both cases, Police and other Government records will indicate if the adult has been deemed unsuitable to work with children.

"Employment" also included the provision of therapy services within those groups but, surprisingly, not that provided privately.

Parents consulting a complementary therapist to obtain therapy for a child, for example, had no way of checking if the therapist had any previous record of misconduct, criminal or otherwise, nor if there were medical grounds why the therapist should not be working with their child.

This loophole is now being closed with the **Safeguarding Vulnerable Groups Act 2006.** This Act, in force from mid-2007, provides for a centralisation of all records and an enhanced Vetting and Barring Scheme.

The Act broadens the types of work that require mandatory CRB checks, and divides them into two categories - Regulated Activity and Controlled Activity.

Regulated Activities include:

- any activity which involves close contact with children or vulnerable adults and is of a specified nature. This includes teaching, training, care and also advice or guidance services;
- any activity allowing contact with children or vulnerable adults and is in a specified place, such as Schools and Care Homes;
- where the activity is frequent (taking place on more than two days in a month) or overnight;
- fostering and childcare;
- certain defined positions of responsibility where children are involved.

Controlled Activities include:

- support work in general health, NHS and Further Education settings;
- those working for specified organisations, such as a Local Authority, and who have access to sensitive records about children;
- support work in adult social care settings.

People wishing to take up such regulated employment need also to be "subject to monitoring", which means that they must be a member of the Vetting and Barring Scheme.

The onus is on the organisation to check that an applicant is a member of the scheme, and if they are not subject to monitoring, or have been barred, then they cannot take up a regulated position.

Under the Act it is an offence for organisations to recruit people to work with children and vulnerable adults that they know are barred. Penalties for doing so can include a prison sentence of up to five years. In addition, failure to make the necessary checks could result in a fine of up to £5000.

The Act also makes it clear that there is no distinction between paid work and voluntary work; if the position involves regulated or controlled activity, then the applicant *must* be subject to monitoring.

More importantly, for the first time domestic employers such as parents will now be able to check whether private tutors, nannies, music teachers, therapists , etc. are barred.

The BTFTA will certainly be looking into the implications of the new law as it relates to the practice of TFT with children. It may be the case that we look towards operating our own validation scheme, perhaps in conjunction with a larger organisation such as the BCMA.

This will no doubt entail some cost for the individual practitioner seeking validation, but we need to be ahead of the game, not following behind, and the investment will reinforce the public perception of TFT as truly professional practice.

Finally, a book recommendation for all of you working or intending to work with children:

Therapy with Children: Children's Rights, Confidentiality and the Law (Ethics in Practice) : SAGE Publications Ltd (March 2000), **ISBN:** 0761952799

This is a "must-read" for a comprehensive consideration of legal and therapeutic issues. The British Journal of Educational Psychology puts it this way:

"This is a thought-provoking book, raising and discussing the important questions that pervade the minefield that is therapy with children. This book is thorough and detailed, referencing many useful and significant legal and official documents by way of answering some of the thorny questions that it raises. This book should prove beneficial for any adults working with children in need of therapeutic support. It carefully highlights the main legal issues and sensitively takes the reader through the process and practice of therapy, and its implications for the psychological well-being of both the client child, and the therapist."

14. Treating Children

1. How to use TFT for treating a Child
2. "Beware of the Child" - Examples & Case Studies
3. Working with Groups of Children

1. How to use TFT for treating a Child

Children love TFT! For very young children you can have some fun and talk about your "**Magic Tapping Game**". This will immediately gain their attention and they will thoroughly enjoy the treatment. When demonstrating tapping the majors on yourself, you can for example also say: "I see" - e, "Monkey" - a, "Tarzan" - c

while fitting the actions to your words!

When you are looking for a SUD, have them show with their hands apart how big the disturbance is for them. (Fear, anger, hurt and so on.) It's the same principle as the size of the fisherman's catch! I once treated a little girl of 5 years old who had come to see me with her daddy because she was suffering from a simple fear. I asked her to show me how big this fear was by stretching out her arms the appropriate amount. She looked at me and then stretched her arms apart as far as they could go. After a quick treatment for the fear I asked how it was now

Thought Field Therapy

and she put her two palms very close and peeped at me through the small gap. Delightful!

Alternatively you could have them point to the chart of smiley faces in the manual. See also chart on page 11.

Other appropriate ideas are: "If your fear was a person - how tall would that person be? " "If it was a Lego building, how high would you make the building? " OR: "Draw as many marbles on a plate as you think you are frightened."

What a difference from talking to the poor little things about some terrible trauma - for example! !

You can also ask the parent or guardian present if they can see the change in the child after the treatment.

2. "Beware of the Child" - Examples & Case Studies

Although I have shown a simple straightforward case with a very young girl, you need to be aware that children come in many different sizes, having very varied mental abilities together with many different problems and past experiences. It is therefore most important to realise that working with children is not always as simple as it would first appear on the surface.

Since 1982, when I first trained in hypnotherapy, I have always specialised in the treatment of children. In 1996 I added TFT to my repertoire of therapeutic approaches, and it rapidly took over as my tool of choice, especially where trauma was involved.

The results were excellent - much better than I'd achieved before - and I rapidly gained an insight into what could and couldn't be treated using TFT.

It also became apparent that the use of TFT in certain circumstances is not required, and could even be hazardous so had to be used with care. Not a fault of TFT, I have to say, but the nature of the presenting problem.

Children love TFT, of course, but a therapist must not be misled into thinking it'll all be plain sailing and that TFT can always solve the problem.

With most children, it can. With some it can't and the solution lies elsewhere. Here's my guide to a few of the oddities and pitfalls...

The "Parent Trainer"

Children don't need wisdom to realise when they are on to a good thing - they function on auto-pilot.

A mother brought her 7 year old son to me because he was "school phobic". She described taking him to school as an absolute nightmare - he'd scream, shout and fight on the way, and if left at the infant school, would cry constantly until his mother came to collect him.

I chatted with the boy for while, asked him to draw pictures of school, asked him what home was like, asked about what he liked, disliked, hated and so on. He was very cooperative and I soon had all the information I needed, especially about Mum...

I then spoke to the mother. "He's not school-phobic", I said, "he's home-philic". Mother looked puzzled. I went on to explain that her son had successfully trained her to be at his beck and call.

She did everything for him - and I really do mean everything. Dressed, fed, toileted, entertained, you name it. Mum had become the source of all pleasure.

At school he had to do things for himself. He hated this and soon discovered that the more upset he became at school the more rewards he would get at home to calm him down.

This was purely Pavlovian in nature, the boy not having wilfully engineered the situation but unconsciously learned his pattern of behaviour. In fact he loved school lessons - and told me so - but as soon as he could not have his own way he kicked off.

Treatment: - nothing for the boy but TFT for mum for her addiction to pandering, some parenting sessions, and some further TFT to deal with her anxiety when her boy screamed. With the help of her sister, who volunteered her support, the boy was rapidly "re-trained" - as was Mum!

The therapeutic lesson? Take a long hard look at the parents and how they bring up their child. The allegedly problematic child may have actually been unwittingly trained to be that way. As there is often nothing wrong with the child, TFT would not work. If you can't offer parenting advice, have a look in Yellow Pages under the Counselling & Advice section.

The "School Phobic"

In my 25 years as a therapist part-time and full-time, I have to say that I have never come across a child who had an irrational fear (i.e. phobia) of school. A much more appropriate term (and it is now more commonly used) is "school refuser".

I can't count the number of school refusers I've dealt with, and the reasons why they were that way were just as numerous. However, one thing did become very clear very quickly - more often than not school refusal begins at home and stays there.

It should be said that there were some immediately obvious non-domestic reasons - bullying, intimidatory teachers, teen relationship angst, and so on - but they were discrete, individual and traumatic in origin, and therefore easily managed.

Even a case where a boy became a refuser because he could not cope emotionally with having his genitals seen by other boys when getting changed for PE! Simple, yet devastating for his school career.

The domestic connection is much more insidious and is closely linked to illness, death or violence within the home.

One case I can describe is of a 12 year old girl whose grandparents had died of heart complaints within weeks of each other. In family discussions she heard her parents speak of the "family legacy" of heart disease and how "it could happen to us at any time".

A casual but impactful remark in conversation but it had a devastating effect on the child. She soon became a school refuser and had been seen by an Educational Psychologist (EP) a number of times with no beneficial outcome.

I do not know why the EP had not picked up on this, but simple questioning of parents, the girl herself and a little bit of lateral thinking, revealed that the girl was terrified to leave home "in case her parents died while she was at school".

Thought Field Therapy

Similar patterns emerge in cases of domestic violence (violent parent might go too far if child is not there as a witness), parental physical illness (child as carer), parental mental illness (child made to feel guilty leaving parent home alone), and more.

Treatment: - TFT for trauma, anxiety, guilt, depression, anger, rage etc. as required for both child and parents, and referral to a family therapist to negotiate a new beginning.

Therapeutic lesson? Don't assume that a "school refusal" is a phobia or fear. Ask searching questions and think carefully about the ecology of the presenting problem, leaving nothing unturned.

The "Attention Seeker"

Usually presenting as parent-identified behaviour problems, it's quite easy this one!

Forget the child for a while and get to grips with the parents. What is it about their parenting that the child sees as neglectful?

Is TV used as a babysitter? Do the parents actually play with the child - or just sit there, and watch the child play? Do the parents listen to the child - not hear, but really listen? I could go on for another few pages...

Treatment: - TFT trauma, anger, rage, depression for the child, the same for the parents plus check for PR when they are thinking about their child. Parenting advice would also be indicated. In the absence of anything to pin the attention seeking upon, i.e. if there is no social perspective, consider environmental toxin exposure.

Therapeutic lesson? The child may not be the problem - never assume he or she is until the ecology of the situation has been explored. However, do remember that the child will be feeling very frustrated and should be treated accordingly.

Finally, a few pitfalls...

Munchausen's Syndrome

Although rare in adults it is surprisingly common in a minor form in children. How many of us faked a "tummy upset" as a child to get attention? !

It only develops into a real problem in childhood if it becomes a chronic occurrence, extends to the child harming themselves, or leads to them becoming subject to unnecessary surgery.

Treatment and therapeutic lesson: - see "Attention Seeker"

Fabricated or Induced Illness

Formerly known as **Munchausen's Syndrome by Proxy**, it is characterised by a person (such as a parent, usually the mother) faking or actually causing a physical or mental illness in another person (such as a child).

This is difficult territory for the complementary therapist. The culprit often chooses such a therapist knowing that their training may be less than comprehensive and is therefore less likely to recognise the truth of the situation. Treatment is offered just on the word of the parent.

I was contacted by a child's mother who was seeking treatment for her child who she said was "not sleeping for fear of the dark".

Thought Field Therapy

On arrival, I spoke at length with the parent and made careful notes of her take on the problem. I then asked the child to come in and her mother to wait outside. I saw the mother stiffen and she immediately refused saying she had to stay with the child.

I explained that I had to be able to talk freely with the child but would leave the door open if the mother wished. Reluctantly, she agreed.

The first comment "Your Mum tells me you don't like the dark" brought the response "Not really", rapidly followed by a voice from outside the room, "Yes, you are darling!" Interesting...

Chatting at length with the child, I could find nothing psychologically abnormal - no monsters, no spooky shadows, nothing that I could find that would go any way to explaining the child's alleged fear. I asked again in a whisper, "Are you really afraid of the dark?" to which the child said "No".

I asked Mum to come back in and gave my opinion. She was not pleased and complained of having come a long way for help.

I knew that TFT treatment would cause no harm in the situation, so I offered to treat the alleged fear directly after provoking some strong thought fields, just in case the child was hiding something.

I began with "the dark closing in" - the child tapped along - and so did Mum, very intensely. I then asked the child to think of "monsters under the bed". The child laughed, and played along but Mum tapped even more intensely.

Then I hit the proverbial nail on the head. "Think about going to sleep and not waking up". Mum froze and burst into tears. I asked the child to leave saying that I'd like to help Mum. "OK", she said - as if this was nothing unusual.

After a while Mum confessed. Nothing wrong with her child, it was her. She said she'd killed her mother in a house fire when she was a child.

Nothing of the kind, of course - further questioning revealed that she'd been traumatised in a house fire in which her mother had indeed died, but she had nothing to do with the fire itself.

Apparently, Mum had seen many therapists over the years to no avail. She'd now taken to seeking out professional help via her child. Whatever therapy was offered to the child she would copy - or take, in the case of homeopathic or herbal remedies. This was why she was so keen to tap along with her child, of course!

I dealt successfully with Mum's presenting trauma, and pointed out that we'd deal with the rest in a couple more appointments. I never saw her or her child again.

I considered notifying Social Services, but it was very apparent that the child was coming to no harm and was delightfully well-balanced mentally, so decided not to. I realise now that this may have been the wrong decision, but I can live with it!

<u>Treatment</u>: - none for the child, just about every algorithm for the mother!

<u>Therapeutic lesson</u>? Ecology again - take a long hard look at the parents as well as the child.

3. Working with Groups of Children

In 2000, I carried out a brief trial project in a Special School. I trained the staff in basic TFT procedures suitable for use on those with learning or behavioural problems.

To be carried out on a one-to-one basis as required, the staff would record subjective assessments of changes occurring in the children they cared for.

Early data indicated that there was a 30% reduction in behaviour associated with frustration and anger, and a similar improvement in "calm time" and concentration.

Unfortunately, the research did not progress into controlled trials as the Local Authority refused to sanction any further work.

I know that taking TFT into schools is an ambition of many TFT practitioners as we well know the benefits that could be brought into the education system if only we could get the break.

Apart from legal hurdles associated with working with children such as Criminal Records Bureau checks, risk assessments and parental permission, I'd also ask you step back and consider the whole ecology (once again!) very carefully.

Most children lead happy, carefree lives with the occasional upset at home or school - nothing serious but enough to upset the child. In these circumstances TFT is ideal - clear out the upset, one happy child again.

However, consider the child who has a less than ideal home life and is regularly traumatised by what goes on under their roof.

Abuse, physical or psychological, takes many direct and indirect forms and children (being great survivors) find ways to suppress their upset, with only minor changes to their behaviour or personality. Teachers usually pick up on the worst cases but many go unnoticed.

It has always amazed me that many abused children will also defend the abusive parent vigorously if challenged. Perhaps this is the child desperately clinging onto the familiar as the lesser of two evils, the second being where they are removed from their parents and taken into a care.

What might happen if such a child was part of a school group or youth club on which an unsuspecting practitioner was demonstrating TFT?

Natural trauma survivors create safe mental havens, often minor phobias, upsets, shyness, reticence and the like to put a lid on the greater upset below.

If we then come along and successfully remove that minor upset through group application of, say, the anxiety or trauma algorithms, the lid of the pressure cooker may then be removed.

Many times have I had such eruptions occur in adults in one-to-one sessions. They present with one or two minor problems and as TFT treatment progresses the metaphorical lid is loosened more and more.

The pressure cooker eventually bursts and a major trauma is revealed. This is challenging enough in a clinical practice situation but imagine it happening in the middle of a class of young children.

Thought Field Therapy

If that child is not in a place of safety or the practitioner is not equipped to handle the outburst that may occur, the consequences for the child and those observing could be devastating.

Needless to say, home circumstances may then be fully revealed and procedures must be in place to manage the eventuality.

We tend to assume that adults will accept this as part of the therapy process, but we cannot do this with children. If we are to take TFT into schools or other youth organisations we will be neglecting our duty of care if we do not give full information about the positives and negatives of TFT treatment to those who remain responsible for what happens to those under their care.

Treatment: - not relevant here, but the practitioner must be fully informed and prepared for all eventualities. The potential for a single negative incident to be blown out of all proportion is high!

Therapeutic lesson? It may be heroic and noble to push and push towards getting TFT accepted within the educational system, but it is even more so to know when to hold back and plan ahead first.

15. Professional Standards

1. The Complementary Medical Practitioner
2. Knowing your limitations
3. The Risks and Duty of Care
4. The Need to Provide a Safe Environment
5. Professional Indemnity Insurance
6. Keeping Records
7. Confidentiality
8. At-a-glance guide

This chapter is intended primarily to help those who have little or no experience of professional practice in any complementary therapy. It is therefore offered as a necessary guide to show what must be followed by any professional practitioner working with the public. Critically this also gives timely warning of legal pitfalls that could occur for the unsuspecting new practitioner due to lack of knowledge of such possibilities.

1. The Complementary Medical Practitioner

Ask the general public what words they would associate with the occupation of Medical Doctor, a typical set would be clever, professional, helpful, responsible, caring, well-trained, etc.

Ask the same for a Complementary Medical Practitioner and these words often appear: strange, odd, weird, hippie, etc. Moreover, ask the general public if they would trust and respect someone practicing Complementary Medicine as much as a Medical Practitioner and the answer is almost always no.

It is still very much the case that anything not understood is ridiculed at best and feared at worst, and despite our present day enlightenment, old myths die hard. People will *try* complementary medicine but will seldom rely on it as much as mainstream medicine.

And they are absolutely right - modern medicine can work its own miracles based on best evidence both in pharmaceuticals and techniques. Antibiotics and modern surgery cannot be surpassed with complementary medicine. Yet for mental health, modern medicine is seen to be lacking - and almost completely dependent on drug-based therapy.

In such cases, complementary medical practitioners enjoy a luxury seldom available to the mainstream - time. Time to listen, time to consider, time to explore. Yet in many of those disciplines, that time can go on and on and on. Weeks, months, even years, with progress but no resolution. The American obsession with psychoanalytic therapy keeps thousands of professionals in riches for their entire working life!

I have to admit to sometimes being a little wicked when, at the start of a TFT training I ask 'quite innocently' a student who is a psychologist or psychoanalyst: "How long do your clients stay in therapy with you? " The answer is usually: "Oh, certainly at least several months, sometimes for a couple of years or so." My reply then:

"Really what you are doing can't be much use, can it? " Perhaps a little unfair, but basically true?

Thought Field Therapists, on the other hand, have the added bonus of using that time at its most efficient, resolving many psychological conditions in a relative instant. The evidence is clear and testable by anyone. Yet distrust and suspicion cloud the view of both the public and the professions.

Although we might like to see this as unduly suspicious of the public, and arguably self-protective on the part of traditional medicine, to reject a technique which holds such potential for the relief of suffering in mankind, it should be appreciated that what we are dealing with is still barely understood by both. Any symptoms created by an action of the mind are still likely to be dismissed as unexplainable, and any "cure" linked to a non-mainstream therapeutic approach, therefore, has to be co-incidental.

The key to acceptance is public and professional confidence and the best way to build confidence in a therapy is to establish standards. Standards are the be all and end all of every profession. Ignore them, or believe that they're fine for some but that there is no need for their rigorous application to everyone, then one comes unstuck very fast. Arrogance has no place in a therapist's make up.

Furthermore, if we, as Thought Field Therapists, think that we are above such things simply because we may actually have at our disposal an approach that is second to none, then we have another think coming.

Nick Adams, a professional Psychologist and Psychotherapist who has worked extensively with all age groups in academic, private and social service sectors, spoke about this issue a few years ago in his inaugural address as Chairman of the British Thought Field Therapy Association.

"In the UK it is possible for anyone to call themselves a therapist (even if they have no training or qualifications whatsoever) as currently there is no statutory regulation of Complementary Medicine. There are exceptions to this - Acupuncture and Osteopathy, to name just two.

Nevertheless, responsible therapists in other fields will ensure that they do follow full and appropriate training in their chosen discipline and the complexities of professional conduct and client care even if it is not a formal requirement.

The Callahans also include very clear advice concerning the practice of TFT in their training materials:

*"The training offered is oriented to providing skills in the rapid treatments developed in Thought Field Therapy. It is **not** intended to provide comprehensive training in the treatment or assistance of those with the problems addressed in this training, nor specialised training in the field of psychology, psychotherapy, or the proper care of patients."*

and

"The purpose of this training is to provide you with the necessary skills to apply TFT to the problems addressed within the scope of your practice, your current license, organisational role, and/or other expertise, and to teach

TFT algorithms to your clients for use in the resolution of their problems."

In the USA, for example, immediate practice of TFT following Algorithm or Diagnostic training is not an issue. Anyone there who wishes to treat others with TFT on a professional basis will already be (or have to become) licensed and have their practice regulated by their relevant State authorities.

In the UK, the position is very different. If anyone chooses to ignore the Callahan's wise words and set up in professional practice immediately after their TFT training with no previous experience as a therapist, there is nothing to prevent them from doing so.

"But TFT should be taught to everyone!" Perhaps it should - there's nothing like it for self-help or dealing with minor problems within a family network.

However, there is a very big difference between learning TFT for use on oneself and with family and friends on a non-professional basis - the "Tapping the Healer Within" approach - and practicing TFT on strangers (fee-paying or not) in a clinical situation.

Remember, one can easily obtain DIY instructions to do just about anything in the home - building a wall, fitting electrical circuits, replacing a boiler, and so on. It saves money, and if you are prepared to accept the consequences of your actions within your own home - go ahead!

What those DIY instructions do **not** do is qualify you as a bricklayer, an electrician or a heating engineer who can then go out and charge others money for a professional service.

The consumer protection industry is constantly fighting a battle against exactly those individuals who, despite evidence to the contrary, regard themselves as "good enough to do the job."

2. Knowing your Limitations

Nick Adams also draws a clear distinction between Psychologist and Psychotherapist.

As a Psychologist one is taught to work within your remit and abide by a rigorous code of conduct, regulated and enforced by bodies charged by Government to oversee the practice

Although voluntary rules also exist for the practice of Psychotherapy, they are monitored and enforced much less vigorously by various governing bodies and it is easier to set your self up as a Psychotherapist - indeed a therapist of any kind - than it is as a Psychologist. In fact, a therapist need not be overseen by any regulatory body and therefore can operate to one's own code of conduct without much fear of challenge. The safety of both therapist and client could be compromised very quickly.

So, for a psychotherapist it is even more important to know, understand and work within your own qualifications, skills and knowledge.

In TFT we have an excellent training structure but, as already mentioned, it does not offer comprehensive training in everything a new therapist should know before going into practice.

Training in setting up a practice, keeping comprehensive client records, taking a case history, therapeutic manner, etc. are the absolute basics for all therapists but for the practice of TFT those basics should also include a good foundation in basic psychological knowledge. This need not extend to full training in psychology but start with a sound understanding of psychological problems that the typical Thought Field Therapist is likely to encounter - and not just picked up from reading about them on the Internet!

The Internet is a great information resource and you can learn a great deal from professionally regulated sites. But the Internet is also largely ***unregulated*** and one can never know for certain that the information given is accurate and up-to-date.

It cannot replace spending serious time studying or going on courses about treating particular psychological problems. It is always helpful to have an accurate and complete picture of a problem to know where TFT can be used effectively and where complementary procedures might also be used.

Even when you know this you should always be prepared to question whether you ***really*** know enough to treat someone.- think carefully about what you are doing, who you are working with and what problems you are treating, then ask yourself, *"Am I the best person to do this? "* There is never anything wrong with referring a client on to those more skilled!

TFT is an incredible therapy and a therapist can be very confident that the chances of harming someone are very low indeed. But this must never, ever extend into overconfidence!

3. The Risks and Duty of Care

The people we see as clients represent all of our clients and we represent all of our colleagues. That is, if we make a mistake in our practice then we not only make ourselves look bad, but also our colleagues. We also put our other clients at risk as they may lose trust in us, and not take the advice that is given to them. This could have a detrimental effect on their therapy.

Additionally, a client may have cause to be unduly worried about the therapy they are receiving, and about the therapist who is treating them, when they should be focusing on their own individual problem.

Of greatest concern, if the therapy that one practices in the community results in mistakes in diagnosis (particularly with therapies still in their infancy) and/or treatment then the public at large will also lose confidence. Many people who could possibly be helped by that therapy will not be treated because of this lack of trust.

We also live in litigious times - a single prosecution could damage the reputation of the therapy for years to come, whether or not the prosecution is successful.

Duty of Care

When working with a client you have a duty of care. In legal terms a duty of care arises when an individual can reasonably foresee that his actions or lack of action could result in harm. Therefore, a duty of care exists between therapist and client because the therapist is providing a service and there is expectation of a certain level of skill, knowledge and expertise.

Once you accept a person as a client you become absolutely committed to helping that person overcome his problems and restore quality to his life. In discharge of this duty we often find ourselves wanting to help everyone and anyone, which is, at one and the same time, a good thing (many otherwise troubled people are helped into new lives) and a bad thing (one becomes a Jack of all trades, yet master of none).

Sometimes, with particularly successful therapies, therapists may develop what might reasonably be called the "God Complex". In other words, they believe they have the skills to help many people, and may well do, but part of the reason they want to help is to satisfy their own psychological or personal needs - to boost their self-esteem, to earn lots of money, to become famous, or even notorious!

They may then believe that they are so good that they can teach other people about how therapy should be done using their methods because of a desire to have people look up to them in admiration. This can only serve to get in the way of being truly open-minded to help the client.

It is perfectly reasonable to want to earn a decent living, or to believe that you are good at something, and if possible develop a new idea or theory.

However it is important to assess and ask ourselves (and, more importantly, to do this under our own supervision) whether we are doing what we do for the right reasons and if what we do is getting in the way of truly helping clients.

Thought Field Therapy

We must ask ourselves these questions on a regular basis. As we know from our own clients, it often takes someone else to point this out to us to really know what it is we are doing.

We need to acknowledge the extent of our capabilities; we need to recognise where our knowledge of TFT has reached its limit; we need to know whether a chosen approach to treatment (whatever it happens to be) is appropriate or not; we need to know what to do when we're absolutely sure that no more perturbations are present and no other factors are having an impact, but the client still has symptoms; we need to have the humility to recognise that we cannot do everything every time.

We do what we do to help our clients - it should never be about us and our personal or psychological needs.

4. The Need to Provide a Safe Environment

This does not refer to your consulting room! It refers to the non-physical environment in which you will work with the client.

If you have a potential client who has a clinically diagnosed or complex problem that you have not worked with before, then either turn down this client and refer them to someone who is qualified, or, within your own supervision, seek out appropriate liaisons with professionals who have experience of this work. Those professionals can advise and guide you as you work your way through the many ramifications of therapy with such clients, and help you fully understand the client's disorder and its effects.

Additionally, provided you have the client's permission to do so, consult the client's GP or Consultant to discuss what you intend to do. Check that there are no contraindications or other problems the client may not have revealed during your initial consultation but that you should be aware of to plan your approach. It is very much a fact of psychotherapeutic practice that those with psychological problems often hide the truth, are "selectively forgetful", or simply tell lies.

But what if the client refuses permission to consult? This should immediately flag up the question "Why? ". If one cannot obtain a completely satisfactory answer then you should turn down the client. If you decide to continue regardless, you could be held to be negligent in your duty of care.

If you have carried out your preliminary consultation, you must then explain to the potential client what you are capable of and, more importantly, what you are not capable of, and make sure that they have read and understood all the implications of the therapy you practice. Client expectations must be very clear. This allows them to make an informed choice as to whether or not they wish to seek your help.

Possibly the worst path you could take is to accept this client just because you think you might be able to help them without really understanding the problem in hand, and / or because you may need an extra bit of income because you haven't seen many clients in the week. This is, beyond any doubt, professionally and ethically wrong and does not provide the client with a truly safe environment.

5. Professional Indemnity Insurance

It is a sad reflection of the lack of regulation of complementary medicine that many therapists are ignorant of the fact that they should be covered by Professional Indemnity Insurance (PII). This puts both therapist and client at risk.

PII provides cover for claims brought against the therapist due to breach of duty, civil liability (breach of contract, libel slander), or negligent acts, errors or omissions in the course of their professional activities.

It should be borne in mind that the insurance cover is not for TFT but for the therapist - even the most competent TFT practitioner could make an error of judgement that may render them liable to civil or criminal action, with awards amounting to millions of pounds.

Some insurance companies also offer cover for "Loss of Reputation". If action is taken against a therapist by a misguided or malicious client and that action is subsequently dismissed, the insurance company will engage the services of a public relations expert to help restore the therapist's reputation as far as possible.

6. Keeping Records

A written record of every consultation should be kept. This is not only good practice in terms of tracking a client's progress, but essential for your defence if a client should decide to litigate against you.

At very least, such records should contain:

- Client's name in full, date of birth and current age.

- Client's postal address and landline telephone number. A mobile number may also be useful but do remember that mobile phones can be switched off, ignored and changed very easily.

- Relevant environmental factors that may affect TFT treatments:

- known allergies and sensitivities

- tobacco use

- recreational drug use

- alcohol consumption in units per day or week.

Sensitive information should be coded in some way so if a record goes astray a third party will not know its meaning. For example AC: 14w could be used for "alcohol consumption: 14 units per week", RDU: Creg, Hocc could be used for "Recreational Drug Use: Cannabis regularly, Heroin occasionally".

- Client consent to receive therapy. This should lay out exactly what the client can expect, together with any limitations and relevant disclaimers. Once the client confirms that they have read and understood its contents they should sign and date it.

- Presenting case. What does the client want therapy for?

Thought Field Therapy

- Case History. Your notes based on questions you ask your client. These must be as thorough as possible. Clinically relevant omissions amount to negligence on your part.

- Case notes. Your notes as treatment progresses, which should contain a minimum of what you did and the client's response, including failures. It is good practice to review these notes as soon as possible after the client has finished a session. It will allow you to see what went well and what didn't, as well as plan ahead for the next session.

- Signing off. Your client's confirmation that therapy is complete. If a client ends therapy before it is complete you must sign it yourself and add a note to that effect together with reasons, if known.

7. Confidentiality

As you might expect you must keep all client information strictly confidential. This does not just include all notes and conversations (including telephone calls and e-mails if they occur), but your opinions too.

Written notes are best as they are not subject to the provisions of the Data Protection Acts. If you wish to keep digital records then you must register with the Information Commissioners Office. In any event, the Freedom of Information Act 2000 allows clients to request a copy of any notes you have made.

Security of records is, of course, paramount. A lockable filing cabinet for their storage is essential, and if computer records are held it would be preferable to encrypt the data.

It is often tempting to talk about clients or cases or offer your opinions of a client with family and friends, on the basis that they will not know the person anyway and you won't be revealing their identity. This is not a professional thing to do under any circumstances. Family and friends are not bound by a code of conduct; they might mention an interesting snippet of what you told them at their place of work, on the bus, over coffee in a café; someone overhears…

Two problems may arise. Firstly, the person who overhears may put two and two together and identify your client from characteristics alone. Secondly, that person will be well within their rights to approach Trading Standards to draw the regulator's attention to the breach of confidentiality.

It is much easier <u>not</u> to talk about your work with anyone who is not directly involved in the client's care. Those directly involved would include yourself and anyone in a similar professional capacity whom you consult as part of your duty of care.

Here's an interesting scenario based on a real-life incident.

You're treating a lady called Mrs. X. There is no need to contact her GP as the case is relatively simple. Two sessions into therapy, you receive a call from Mrs. X's GP to discuss her progress. He tells you she's given him permission to know what you've been doing. What do you do?

Those who answered *"share the information as it's the professional thing to do"* go to the bottom of the class.

Mrs. X's GP? How do you know? Could it be her estranged husband, a newspaper reporter, a solicitor, a debt collector, all wanting information that Mrs. X would not want anyone else to know?

So, how do you handle such a thing? You can't even say that you'll have to verify the request with Mrs. X first. Why? Because you've then just given away the fact that she's consulting you - a breach of confidentiality and your duty of care!

The words to use go something like this*: "Thanks for calling, but if I were to be treating someone with that name, they'd expect complete confidentiality, so I really can't help you."*

You've given nothing away, and you can then contact Mrs. X to get her side of the story. If the caller is genuine, they'll understand and end the call. If the caller is insistent, simply repeat that you have explained why you cannot help and hang up.

Another scenario: You're on a shopping trip and you see Mrs. X approaching. What do you do?

Say "hello"? Smile and say "how are you"? Nod your head and acknowledge her presence?

Answer: none of the above. Even a glance and slight smile or nod confirms that you either know or are acquainted with Mrs. X. What if Mrs. X is with someone who then asks her "Who's that"?

If Mrs. X acknowledges you first, it's a different matter! But best prepare your nonchalant walk-on-by for future use.

And one more: You treat a person with great success and in their gratitude they say that they're happy to have their name mentioned to promote your practice. What do you do?

If you get this one wrong then you really need to reinforce your understanding of duty of care. The answer: never, ever, under any circumstances, reveal a client's real name even if they say that you can. You risk alienating potential clients who fear that you may use their name in publicity too. Of course, you'll never do this without their permission - but they don't know that because they've never even bothered calling you.

8. At-a-glance guide

The following guide to the professional standards that a therapist is expected to meet is based on those published in a typical contract for a non-medically qualified practitioner providing services within the NHS.

1. **Qualifications:** Practitioners should be in receipt of a recognised qualification from a training establishment which is accredited by a suitable regulatory body.

2. **Registration:** Practitioners must be registered with a recognised professional body which requires its members to abide by codes of conduct, ethics and discipline.

3. **Insurance:** Practitioners must have adequate professional indemnity insurance cover that applies to the period of their employment.

4. **Consent to treatment:** Patients must be fully informed about the nature of the therapy and its effects, including any side effects, and have realistic expectations of its benefits. The informed consent of the patient or, in the case of young children, of the parent or guardian, must be gained and documented.

5. **Medical responsibility**: Practitioners should be aware that patients referred to them for treatment remain the overall responsibility of the referring clinician. CAM practitioners should not advise discontinuing existing orthodox treatments without the agreement of the referring clinician.

6. **Documentation:** A written record should be kept by practitioners of the consultation and each episode of treatment. All written (and oral information) should be treated as confidential and take account of the needs of the Data Protection Act and Caldecott review.

7. **Refusal to treat:** Practitioners have a duty not to treat a patient if they consider the treatment unsafe or unsuitable.

8. **Education and training:** Practitioners should take responsibility for keeping abreast of developments in the practice of their therapy.

9. **Quality Standards:** Practitioners, in conjunction with other health care professionals, should assist with the development of local standards and guidelines for practice.

10. **Audit:** Practitioners should be responsible for monitoring and recording the outcome of therapy; opinions of patients should be actively sought and included in any evaluation.

11. **Research:** Practitioners should be expected to agree to take part in research trials to support the evaluation and development of treatment programmes.

12. **Health and safety:** Practitioners should comply with the requirements of Health and Safety legislation and adhere to good practice in the protection of staff, patients and the public.

Appendix 1

Abbreviations for TFT Algorithm Treatment Points

e	under eye (under the pupil just below the rim of the bone)
a	under arm (about 10cm down from the arm pit; at the bra line for women)
c	collarbone (2-3cm down from the V of the neck and 2-3cm over to either left or right)
eb	inside eyebrow (at the point where the eyebrow begins)
tf	tiny (little) finger (the tip beside the nail on the thumb side)
if	index finger (the tip beside the nail on the thumb side)
oe	outside edge of eye (about 1cm straight out from the corners of the eyes, on the edges of the bones of the eye sockets)
un	under nose (central on the upper lip)
ch	chin (in the cleft between the chin and lower lip)
g	gamut spot (between the knuckles of the little and ring finger about ½ inch back onto the hand)
s/h	side of hand (between base of little finger and wrist)

SUD   subjective units of distress (a rating on a scale of 0-10 or 1-10 of how upset one is at the moment)

9 Gamut Sequence

While continuously tapping the gamut spot carry out the following procedure:

1. eyes closed
2. eyes open
3. eyes moved down to one side
4. eyes moved down to other side
5. roll eyes in a complete circle
6. roll eyes in a complete circle the other way
7. <u>hum</u> a few bars of a tune (aloud)
8. count from one to five (aloud)
9. <u>hum</u> again (aloud)

er   floor-to-ceiling eye roll (while tapping the gamut spot, hold head level, look down to the floor, slowly to a count of 10, roll your eyes vertically upwards to the ceiling).

Appendix 2

Collarbone Breathing Exercise cb²

This is occasionally needed when it is found that a normally successful treatment fails to work or hold for a significant length of time. In the case of addiction treatment this procedure needs to be carried out regularly. It is also an excellent stress-reliever for use at any time.

<u>Touch the collarbone points in the following order:</u>

- Two fingers of one hand touching one of the collarbone points

    ⇨ Follow treatment instructions below

- The same two fingers touching the other collarbone point

    ⇨ Follow treatment instructions below

- Two knuckles of that hand touching one of the collarbone points

    ⇨ Follow treatment instructions below

- The same two knuckles touching the other collarbone point

    ⇨ Follow treatment instructions below

- Two fingers of the other hand touching one of the collarbone points

    ⇨ Follow treatment instructions below

- The same two fingers touching the other collarbone point

    ⇨ Follow treatment instructions below
- Two knuckles of that hand touching one of the collarbone points

    ⇨ Follow treatment instructions below
- The same two knuckles touching the other collarbone point

    ⇨ Follow treatment instructions below

Treatment Instructions:

1. Begin tapping the gamut spot of the hand in contact with the collarbone point and breathe normally for a while. Then keep tapping, allowing for 5-10 taps at each hold, whilst doing the following breathing movements:
2. Take a **deep breath** in - hold a few seconds...
3. Breathe **halfway** out - hold a few seconds...
4. Breathe **all the way** out - hold a few seconds...
5. Breathe **halfway** in - hold a few seconds...
6. Rest, change to next position.

Summary

One Hand: Fingers, Fingers, Knuckles, Knuckles. Tap and Breathe at each point

Other Hand: Fingers, Fingers, Knuckles, Knuckles. Tap and Breathe at each point

Printed in Great Britain
by Amazon